BARRON'S BOOK NOTES

J. D. SALINGER'S

Catcher in the Rye

BY

Joseph Claro

SERIES EDITOR

Michael Spring
Editor, *Literary Cavalcade*
Scholastic Inc.

BARRON'S EDUCATIONAL SERIES, INC.

ACKNOWLEDGMENTS
We would like to acknowledge the many painstaking hours of work Holly Hughes and Thomas F. Hirsch have devoted to making the *Book Notes* series a success.

All inquiries should be addressed to:
Barron's Educational Series, Inc.
250 Wireless Boulevard
Hauppauge, New York 11788

Library of Congress Catalog Card No. 84-18496

International Standard Book No. 0-8120-3407-4

Library of Congress Cataloging in Publication Data
Claro, Joseph.
J. D. Salinger's Catcher in the rye.

(Barron's book notes)
Bibliography: p. 85
Summary: A guide to reading "Catcher in the Rye" with a critical and appreciative mind. Includes background on the author's life and times, sample tests, term paper suggestions, and a reading list.
1. Salinger, J. D. (Jerome David), 1919– Catcher in the rye.
[1. Salinger, J.D. (Jerome David), 1919– . Catcher in the rye.
2. American literature—History and criticism] I. Title.
PS3537.A426C323 1984 813'.54 84-18496
ISBN 0-8120-3407-4 (pbk.)

PRINTED IN THE UNITED STATES OF AMERICA

67890 550 1098

CONTENTS

ADVISORY BOARD

We wish to thank the following educators who helped us focus our *Book Notes* series to meet student needs and critiqued our manuscripts to provide quality materials.

HOW TO USE THIS BOOK

You have to know how to approach literature in order to get the most out of it. This *Barron's Book Notes* volume follows a plan based on methods used by some of the best students to read a work of literature.

Begin with the guide's section on the author's life and times. As you read, try to form a clear picture of the author's personality, circumstances, and motives for writing the work. This background usually will make it easier for you to hear the author's tone of voice, and follow where the author is heading.

Then go over the rest of the introductory material—such sections as those on the plot, characters, setting, themes, and style of the work. Underline, or write down in your notebook, particular things to watch for, such as contrasts between characters and repeated literary devices. At this point, you may want to develop a system of symbols to use in marking your text as you read. (Of course, you should only mark up a book you own, not one that belongs to another person or a school.) Perhaps you will want to use a different letter for each character's name, a different number for each major theme of the book, a different color for each important symbol or literary device. Be prepared to mark up the pages of your book as you read. Put your marks in the margins so you can find them again easily.

Now comes the moment you've been waiting for—the time to start reading the work of literature. You may want to put aside your *Barron's Book Notes* volume until you've read the work all the way through. Or you may want to alternate, reading the *Book Notes* analysis of each section as soon as you have finished reading the corresponding part of the original. Before you move on, reread crucial passages you don't fully understand. (Don't take this guide's analysis for granted—make up your own mind as to what the work means.)

Once you've finished the whole work of literature, you may want to review it right away, so you can firm up your ideas about what it means. You may want to leaf through the book concentrating on passages you marked in reference to one character or one theme. This is also a good time to reread the *Book Notes* introductory material, which pulls together insights on specific topics.

When it comes time to prepare for a test or to write a paper, you'll already have formed ideas about the work. You'll be able to go back through it, refreshing your memory as to the author's exact words and perspective, so that you can support your opinions with evidence drawn straight from the work. Patterns will emerge, and ideas will fall into place; your essay question or term paper will almost write itself. Give yourself a dry run with one of the sample tests in the guide. These tests present both multiple-choice and essay questions. An accompanying section gives answers to the multiple-choice questions as well as suggestions for writing the essays. If you have to select a term paper topic, you may choose one from the list of suggestions in this book. This guide also provides you with a reading list, to help you when you start research for a term paper, and a selection of provocative comments by critics, to spark your thinking before you write.

THE AUTHOR AND HIS TIMES

J. D. Salinger shares at least one important trait with his character Holden Caulfield—a powerful urge to separate himself from society.

Holden, the chief character of *The Catcher in the Rye,* tells us that he wants to live on the edge of the woods; Salinger realized this dream by retreating to a small farm town in New Hampshire, where the townspeople seem as devoted to his privacy as he is himself. There, in Cornish, Salinger has been able to escape the distractions of the literary world and to avoid people who have sought to capitalize on his instant fame following the publication of *The Catcher in the Rye* in 1951.

Little is known about Salinger's life since he moved to Cornish. Local residents enjoy protecting Salinger's anonymity, and interviews with them typically have produced bland, noncommittal responses that make Salinger sound about as interesting as last month's newspaper. Salinger himself refuses to be interviewed.

The facts of Salinger's earlier life, however, are on the record. Jerome David Salinger was born in New York City in 1919, the son of a prosperous importer of meat and cheese. He was a mediocre student in the public school he attended, and after he flunked out of the private McBurney School, his parents sent him to Valley Forge Military Academy in Pennsylvania.

He later spent less than a month at New York University and then took a short-story course at Columbia University. His first story was published in 1940.

From 1942 to 1946 he was in the Army, continuing to write "whenever I can find time and an unoccupied foxhole." He returned to New York in 1946, and in the next few years had stories published in various periodicals, notably *The New Yorker.*

In 1953 Salinger met Claire Douglas, a British-born Radcliffe student. She apparently became the model for more than one of his characters. They were married two years later, and they have two children, Margaret Ann, born in 1955, and Matthew, born in 1960. They were divorced in 1967.

Salinger's later published works have all been stories. Most of them deal with the children of the Glass family, who, like Salinger, have a Jewish father and a Christian mother. These stories have been collected in *Nine Stories* (1953); *Franny and Zooey* (1961); and *Raise High the Roof Beam, Carpenters and Seymour: An Introduction* (1963). All three books received considerable critical praise and were very popular.

Salinger's published literary output declined over the years. By the early 1980s, he had not published a work in some twenty years. Still, he is considered one of the most vital writers of the century. His reputation rests largely on *The Catcher in the Rye.*

In Chapter 12 of *The Catcher in the Rye,* Holden Caulfield is at a bar listening to a jazz piano player whose work he enjoys. The applause from the audience, and the musician's acceptance of it, lead Holden to say: "I swear to God, if I were a piano player or an actor or something and all those dopes thought I was terrific, I'd hate it. I wouldn't even want them to *clap* for me. . . . I'd play it in the goddam closet."

When you think of the life that Salinger chose while he was still a young man with a promising literary future, you realize that these sentences express his worldview as much as Holden's. Careful readers of Salinger's fiction have found many other statements that might also be the sentiments of a man who deserted fame in order to be able to work on his own.

It's not only the feelings about fame that the author and his character have in common. Salinger has often said that children are the best people he knows, a statement that Holden would happily echo. Salinger left New York City primarily because he found its literary circles at best unsatisfying; Holden can't stand being surrounded by phonies everywhere he goes.

Salinger grew up in New York City, and so did Holden. Salinger went to a prep school, and so does Holden. Like Holden, Salinger was a bright child whose grades in school were not an accurate reflection of his intelligence. It's clear from *The Catcher in the Rye* and his other works that Salinger is one of those writers whose works seem to flow directly from experience. He tends to write about familiar territory. But this is far from saying that his characters are strictly autobiographical.

In addition, this kind of information is of less importance to a reader of the novel than it is to a biographer. If you were doing research for a biography of Salinger, it could be vital for you to learn that one of his characters was based on a real person. But it's almost irrelevant to an enjoyment of the novel.

To many contemporary readers encountering it for the first time, *The Catcher in the Rye* fits neatly into a classification called Young Adult Fiction. This is a category that includes serious novels dealing with teenage characters, and written with a teenage reading audience in mind.

Lumping Salinger's book together with thousands of others in this category, however, doesn't do justice to *The Catcher in the Rye.* When the book was published in 1951, there was no such category as Young Adult Fiction. Salinger attracted the attention of the reading audience because he was breaking new ground.

Not only did *The Catcher in the Rye* have a teenager for a central character; he spoke in a manner that was easily recognizable as genuine, and he talked about matters that were serious enough to make even the most complacent reader a bit uncomfortable. One of those matters was his inability to fit into the world of adults.

Such books may be very common today, but in 1951 a teenager talking about his innermost concerns was considered a somewhat eccentric literary device—a reviewer for *The New York Times* didn't even take the book seriously.

Salinger's novel was definitely a groundbreaker in its field. As you read it, try to envision the impact this novel had on its first readers back in 1951. If you're like most readers then, you'll learn much about yourself as well as about Holden Caulfield as you explore the world of *The Catcher in the Rye.*

THE NOVEL

The Plot

If you think of a plot as a series of events that build one on another toward a climax, then the plot of *The Catcher in the Rye* is one of its least significant aspects. It can be summarized in a few paragraphs, but the summary will give only an indication of what the novel is about.

Holden Caulfield is a sixteen-year-old prep school student who has flunked out of school the week before Christmas. Several days before he's expected home for Christmas vacation, he leaves school, planning to spend some time on his own in New York City, where he lives.

Though Holden is friendly with many people at school, and though he has several friends in New York, he's constantly lonesome and in need of someone who will sympathize with his feelings of alienation.

The person Holden feels closest to is his ten-year-old sister, Phoebe, but he can't call her for fear of letting his parents know he has left school. He spends his time with a variety of people, but he can't make meaningful contact with any of them.

After a day of this futility, he sneaks into his home to see Phoebe, but she disappoints him by being annoyed at his being expelled from still another school. Holden decides that the only solution to his overwhelming problem is to run away and establish a new identity as a deaf mute who will not need to communicate with anyone.

On the verge of a nervous collapse, Holden changes his mind and decides to rejoin his family. He then enters a hospital or rest home not far from Hollywood, California, and he is telling us his story while in this institution. At the novel's close, Holden isn't sure whether he'll be able to handle things better when he leaves the institution, and he's sorry he told his story at all.

Those are the bare bones of the story, but there's much more to *The Catcher in the Rye* than its story. It's a rich psychological portrait of a boy who's frightened at the prospect of growing up, a boy who has few of the tools necessary to face the world on his own.

Although the book takes place during only three days, it is as much an autobiography as anything else, because Holden constantly digresses to tell us about things that happened long before this period in his life. Because of Salinger's skill in describing someone in just a few sentences, we also meet several characters who are instantly recognizable.

The Catcher in the Rye has an intriguing story. And it also contains marvelous character portraits; a statement on the relationship of outsiders to society; a psychological analysis of the process of growing up; and many more things, which you'll discover as you read it.

The Characters

Holden Caulfield

Holden is the sixteen-year-old son of wealthy parents who live near Central Park in New York City. He is telling the story from a rest home or hospital near Hollywood. Holden has just flunked out of his third prep school, an event he tries without success to feel badly about. Because of his age, school should be the most important institution in his life, but Holden has no use for it. Although he's intelligent and fairly well read, school represents repression to him; it stands for the "phony" standards and values he hates.

Holden is sensitive, probably too sensitive for his own good, and he suffers from an almost uncontrollable urge to protect people he sees as vulnerable. He is attracted to the weak and the frail, and he "feels sorry for" losers of all kinds, even those who cause him pain, discomfort, or trouble. But the main focus of Holden's protective instinct is children, whom he sees as symbols of goodness and innocence, and whom he would like to shield against corruption.

One sign of corruption in Holden's worldview is the process of growing up, since it removes us from the perfect innocence of childhood. He has a daydream about children who never grow up, who remain in that perfect world forever, and his own problems of facing the real world are linked to that daydream.

Holden is essentially a loner, but not because he dislikes people. His loneliness arises from the fact that no one seems to share his view of the world, no one understands what's going on in his head. His poor academic record is one indication of his failure to deal with this problem, a problem that builds to a climax in the course of the novel.

Phoebe Caulfield

Phoebe is Holden's ten-year-old sister, a bright and articulate girl who sometimes talks to Holden as though she were older than he. She's one of the few people he feels great affection for, and he talks about her with obvious delight. She's the personification of Holden's idealized view of childhood, and she seems actually to possess all the wonderful qualities Holden ascribes to her. The problem for Holden is that she's a real person, not an idealization, and she's already showing signs of the process of growing up. Phoebe appears in person very late in the book, but she plays a central role in Holden's thoughts, and has much influence on what happens to him at the end of the novel.

Allie Caulfield

Allie was Holden's younger brother. He died in 1946, three years before the events in the novel. As with Phoebe, Holden has idealized the brother he loved very much; unlike Phoebe, Allie's personality is frozen in memory, and he'll never face the corruption of growing up. Holden talks about Allie in the same loving terms he uses for Phoebe, and he even talks to his dead brother in moments of stress.

D.B. Caulfield

D.B. is Holden's older brother, another family character we never see, although Holden mentions him often. In the book's opening paragraph Holden tells us that D.B. is a writer of short stories who's now "out in Hollywood . . . being a prostitute"—that is, not being an honest writer.

Mrs. Caulfield

Holden's mother makes a brief appearance late in the book, but we never see her together with her son. She appears to be a high-strung woman, a condition Holden relates to Allie's death. She seems not to be very interested in Phoebe's activities, and the same is probably true of Holden's.

Mr. Caulfield

We never see Mr. Caulfield, and we know very little about him. He's a successful corporation lawyer. His interest in Holden's welfare extends at least far enough for him to have discussed the matter recently with one of Holden's former teachers.

Jane Gallagher

Jane is a girl Holden spent the summer with eighteen months before the start of the story. Though she's about two years older than he is, her shyness and insecurity awakened Holden's protective instincts. She symbolizes innocence in Holden's mind, as Phoebe and Allie do. Holden hasn't seen Jane since that summer, but he remembers her fondly as the shy girl who kept all her kings in the back row when they played checkers. Although she never appears in the book, she helps precipitate the book's first crisis, when Holden's womanizing roommate has a date with her. Holden talks about contacting her throughout the book, but he never does.

Ward Stradlater

Stradlater, Holden's roommate at school, is likable and outgoing, handsome, athletic, and very attractive to girls. He's not sensitive to people's feelings, and in Holden's mind he represents a class of successful people who live by false values and take advantage of others. Holden becomes very upset when he learns that Stradlater has a date with Jane Gallagher, and the situation ends in a fist fight.

Robert Ackley

Ackley lives in the room next to Holden's at school. He's consistently nasty. Holden understands that Ackley's offensiveness stems from insecurity, but that doesn't make him any easier to get along with.

Sally Hayes

Sally is a good-looking but shallow girl Holden has dated in the past, and one of several people to whom he reaches out for help. Like Stradlater, Sally represents the phony values Holden hates, but her physical attractiveness leads Holden to put his principles aside. He tries to explain to her what's happening in his life, but she's incapable of relating to his problems. Even though he hates everything she stands for, Holden proposes marriage to her in a moment of extreme weakness.

Carl Luce

Luce is a college student who used to be a senior adviser to Holden when they both attended the same prep school. Luce was notorious for holding discussions on sex with younger students; Holden suspects he might be a homosexual. Though Holden hasn't seen him in a long time, he calls Luce in his desperate need to talk to someone.

Mr. Spencer

Mr. Spencer, an older history teacher at Pencey Prep, is concerned about Holden's academic failure. He invites Holden to his home to talk things over, but the conversation is a disaster. Though Spencer's concern is genuine, he doesn't have an inkling of what Holden is like, and all he can offer are clichés and slogans as advice.

Mr. Antolini

Mr. Antolini is a former English teacher of Holden's. Like Spencer, he's concerned about Holden's welfare, but his interest is more personal than Spencer's. (At one point Holden thinks it's *too* personal.) Antolini is young and understanding, and he seems to have an idea of what's bothering Holden.

Other Elements

SETTING

The physical action of the book takes place in 1949 at two locations. The first seven chapters—about one quarter of the book—are set at Pencey Prep, a private school for boys in eastern Pennsylvania. Then Holden takes a train ride, and the rest of the book takes place in New York City.

New York City, though, isn't a very accurate description of the major setting. It's actually Manhattan, but even that doesn't narrow it down enough, because Holden's adventures take him through only a fraction of Manhattan, a section less than four miles long and probably half as wide.

Add to this the fact that Holden gives very little description of most of the places where he goes, and you have a novel that seems to have no real setting. But that isn't the case at all.

In the first place, Holden gives some description of each place he's in, but he does it in the casual, throwaway manner that characterizes most of his speech. It's so casual, in fact, that you may not even be aware of reading a descriptive passage.

Second, Holden describes his surroundings when they're important to him. You may find yourself looking forward to visiting the American Museum of Natural History after he's told you about it. He paints a memorable picture of the carousel in Central Park when Phoebe decides to take a ride. He does the same for Fifth Avenue on a shopping day before Christmas.

These descriptions are less important than in most novels. *The Catcher in the Rye* could take place almost anywhere in the United States (and in many places throughout the world). That's because the true setting of the book is Holden's mind. Critics say such a book is an interior monologue or that it employs the stream-of-consciousness technique.

So many incidents in *The Catcher in the Rye* took place before the weekend we're spending with Holden, so much of what has deeply affected him happened years earlier, and such an important part of his life goes on inside his head, that the present physical setting becomes almost incidental to the story being told.

As for the time the story takes place, don't even think about it during your first reading. (There's a good chance that you'll want to read it again.) Except for a few minor references, which are pointed out as they appear in the story (see The Story section of this guide), the book reads as though it were written very recently. That's one of the reasons why people are still reading it after all these years.

THEMES

When you're talking about a novel that says something significant about how people live, it's a mistake to use a sentence that begins, "The theme of this novel is . . . " A good novel doesn't have only one theme. Good novels are about many things and have several themes.

The Catcher in the Rye is no exception. It can be read in several different ways, and every reading can be rewarding. You might get one message from your first reading and an entirely different message from a second reading five or ten years from now.

Here are some statements that have been made about the novel. Think about them as you read. After you've finished, decide how accurate you think each of them is in capturing the essence of the book.

1. It is a novel about a disturbed teenager. Holden can't cope with people, with school, or with everyday problems that people his age must face. He avoids reality by living a fantasy life, and every forced contact with reality drives him deeper into himself. According to this analysis, he is anything but a typical teenager, and he certainly isn't a good role model for young people.

2. It is about a teenager who refuses to grow up. He has a fixation on childhood, which shows itself in his glorifying of children, his inordinate admiration of his younger sister, his idealization of his dead younger brother, and the joy he gets from reminiscing about his own childhood. He brings on his illness so he won't have to face his approaching adulthood.

3. It is a comment on the insensitivity of modern society. Holden is a hero who stands against the false standards and hypocrisy that almost all others accept. As much as he would like to accept the world and be comfortable like almost everyone else, he can't pretend that his society is worthwhile.

4. It is a comic novel about the way the adult world appears to an intelligent literate teenager. Holden subjects everyone he meets to a probing examination, and almost everyone fails. His comments are more about human nature in general than about individual people, which helps explain why the book remains popular.

5. It is about a boy who struggles to remain faithful to what he sees as the truth. His version of truth, however, is very subjective, and not necessarily correct. In his mind even good or beautiful things can be tainted because of the true motives of their creators.

STYLE

In one sense, Salinger was trying to capture the speech patterns of a typical teenager of the 1950s. But language reveals character, and the manner in which Holden expresses himself also gives us many important insights into his personality. His loose, rambling expressions reflect his own inner confusion. He often seems unwilling or afraid to say exactly what he feels, first, because he doesn't know what he feels, and, second, because he's afraid of revealing himself to a world that is either indifferent to him or ready to tear him apart. His language is trite, imprecise, and imitative because of his own lack of self-definition, and because of his inability or unwillingness to communicate with others. His use of the word "really" (as in "It really is") and his repetition of the expression, "if you want to know the truth," reflect his commitment to sincerity, and his drive to dissociate himself from the so-called phonies, who use language to hide from their feelings.

As you read, you'll notice that Salinger frequently italicizes words. This is part of his attempt to accurately duplicate speech patterns—an italicized word is one that is emphasized or stressed when spoken. (Remember that the whole book is really a monologue—an *interior* monologue—spoken by Holden.) Salinger was one of the first writers in English to frequently use italics to indicate regular spoken emphasis—not just a loud voice or a scream. Many writers have since used the technique.

POINT OF VIEW

As is generally true of a work of fiction told in the first person, we learn about all the events and characters through the eyes of the narrator. This subjective point of view has added significance in *The Catcher in the Rye*. "The setting of the book," we suggested on page 14 of this guide, "is Holden's mind." The point of view is an integral part of Salinger's exploration of that mind. The first-person narration invites a reader to share Holden's feeling that he's an outsider observing a world he can't accept—or completely reject. The reader should be aware, however, that the narration is slanted and may not report matters accurately.

FORM AND STRUCTURE

Holden tells his story in a series of flashbacks, or digressions. There is nothing logical or orderly about the way a person's memory works, and so Holden's mind drifts in and out of the past, dwelling on moments that often seem to bear little relationship to each other. Like a patient on a psychiatrist's couch, he lets his mind take him where it will. One memory—one emotion—triggers another, and it's up to us as readers to try to discover the relationship between them.

Some readers have suggested that these flashbacks signify Holden's inability to deal with the world he lives in. Others say they reflect his introspective personality; still others say they are a sign that Holden's grip on reality is loosening, and that he can no longer distinguish between past and present.

While you're reading *The Catcher in the Rye* it's easy to forget that Holden is telling the story from a hospital bed, and that he's there because of the events he tells us about in the book. In the first paragraph of the novel he says that these events "happened to me around last Christmas just before I got pretty run-down and had to come out here and take it easy." It isn't until the last chapter of the book that we see another reference to the place where he's recuperating.

This hospital (or rest home) setting is the overall structure on which the story is built. Some people have said that Salinger used this structure to identify Holden as a misfit, a person who can't cope, someone who needs professional help to deal with life's problems.

Others have said that this structure simply sets Holden apart from everything he's experienced, that it distances him from the people and events he tells us about.

Within that structure the story itself divides neatly into three parts. The first part has Holden at Pencey, preparing to leave on his own before he's formally expelled.

In this first section Holden tells us about two of the three important people in his life—his dead brother Allie and Jane Gallagher. Although she never appears, Jane plays an important role in this section because she's on a date with Holden's roommate. In fact, you could argue that the fight he has over her with his roommate is the real reason he decides to leave school on Saturday night.

Chapter 8 serves as a transition from Pencey to New York City. The second part of the book, which begins with Chapter 9, has Holden trying to find someone he can talk honestly with, someone he can make contact with, someone who will understand what's bothering him.

This is also the section in which we learn about Phoebe, the other important person in Holden's life. By the end of this section, in Chapter 20, Holden is more alone than ever before, he's close to hysteria, and he's thinking about what a relief death would be.

When Holden decides to go home and visit Phoebe, the novel enters the third and final section. In this section Holden has to face some ugly truths that he's been trying hard to avoid—truths about his sister, about childhood innocence, and about himself.

When the third section reaches a climax in Chapter 25 we're abruptly brought back to the outside structure of the novel, the bed from which Holden is speaking. It's in this outside structure, from a vantage point several months and several thousand miles away, that Holden makes his final comments on the whole matter.

The Story

CHAPTER 1

Who is this person talking to us so casually in the opening sentences of the novel? We don't know his name, how old he is, where he's from. In fact, he dismisses such information as "all that David Copperfield kind of crap," and begins talking about himself reluctantly, as though our need to hear his story is much stronger than his need to tell it.

We don't even know it's a boy talking until he mentions an ad his school runs in "about a thousand magazines" claiming that they turn boys into young men. We won't know his first name until his visit to a teacher at the end of the chapter, and we'll have to wait even longer to find out his last name.

No, he isn't going to give us anything as formal as an autobiography. All he wants to do is tell about "this madman stuff" that resulted in some kind of illness, from which he's now recuperating in a place not far from Hollywood, California.

NOTE: As you read on and get to know Holden, you'll begin to see that he tends to dismiss many important things with throwaway phrases like "this madman stuff." It's a way of downplaying things that bother him; it makes him seem untroubled by things; it's a way of sounding tough, something that's important to many teenage boys.

Holden talks briefly about his brother, D.B., whom he obviously admires. He's pleased that his brother visits him often. He likes D.B.'s sports car and the fact that he's rich, and Holden's really proud of a published collection of D.B.'s short stories. But a tough guy can't say things like that about someone without backing off a little, so Holden ends by saying that his brother is in Hollywood, being a prostitute—using his talent to make money, instead of creating beautiful stories.

We get all this information—directly or by implication—in a single paragraph. As is often true with people we've just met, the way Holden talks tells us at least as much about him as what he says. His language tells us that he doesn't want to be mistaken for someone soft, even when he's expressing affection for his brother.

His language also tells us that he doesn't want to be thought of as one of those "splendid, clear-thinking young men" his school claims to mold. Sure, he's read Dickens' novel *David Copperfield*, and you'll soon find that he's read—and appreciated—much more than that. But he doesn't want anyone to think he's a "brain," so he'll remind you from time to time what a terrible student he is.

As he begins his story about the "madman stuff," Holden is standing alone on a hill, looking down at a football game attended by almost everyone from his school. He's wearing a red hunting hat that further sets him apart from everyone else at school. Hold onto this image of him as a loner, apart from the group he's supposed to belong to. It will help you understand much of what is to come.

One of the reasons Holden is alone during the football game is that he's preparing himself for an unpleasant chore. He's going to visit his history teacher before leaving for Christmas vacation, because he isn't coming back to school.

"I forgot to tell you about that," he adds casually. "They kicked me out."

This is another example of the way Holden tries to distract attention (his as well as yours) from large issues. Being expelled from school would be an important event in anyone's life, and you'll see that it's one of the causes of "this madman stuff" Holden says he's going to tell us about. Yet he tells us he "forgot" to mention it.

Holden fires a couple of generalizations at us in this chapter. You might want to stop and think about them, because he does this throughout the book.

The first kind of generalization is the one he uses when he's trying to make a point, the kind someone would use in an argument. Somebody stole his expensive coat and gloves, and he tells us it's the type of thing you'd expect at Pencey. "The more expensive a school is, the more crooks it has," he concludes. This kind of generalization is usually amusing, because it's an overstatement. But it also often has some truth to it.

The second kind of generalization Holden frequently uses may sometimes puzzle you and at other times have you saying, "Right! I know *exactly* what he means!" There's an example of it when he's talking about running to Mr. Spencer's house: "It was that kind of a crazy afternoon," he says, "terrifically cold, . . . and you felt like you were disappearing every time you crossed a road."

Exactly what is Holden talking about when he says something like that? He's describing a very personal, private feeling he's had, maybe more than once, and he's trying to make it sound like something everyone experiences.

Probably no one has experienced exactly what he's referring to, but you might have had that type of feeling. So, even if his details sound a bit strange, the point he's making with these generalizations usually comes across clearly.

NOTE: Think about how much information Salinger has packed into this seemingly informal opening chapter. Holden may appear to be rambling, giving you random tidbits about himself and constantly wandering off into digressions. But consider how much you already know about him:

- He's in a health facility, being treated for a condition that probably resulted from "all this madman stuff," and that might have been complicated by a close brush with tuberculosis ("I practically got t.b.").
- The comments he makes at the very beginning about his parents tell you he probably doesn't get along very well with them.
- His camel's-hair coat and the fact that he goes to Pencey tell you his family has money. The fact that he feels it necessary to mention that the Spencers don't have a maid tells you that his family may be quite wealthy.
- His reaction to Selma Thurmer suggests that he's willing to delve beneath someone's appearance or outward behavior, though he might deny that because it doesn't sound tough.
- His willingness to visit a teacher he'll never see again—as much as he doesn't want to go—suggests a sense of responsibility.

Other things are also hinted at in the first chapter. If you take another look at it you'll discover things that are subtly suggested, rather than stated outright.

Salinger is aiming here for a true-to-life, three-dimensional portrait of a teenager many of us recognize. Holden doesn't especially want to tell us about himself, so we have to find out a great deal indirectly. Salinger's success depends partly on how intelligently you read what he has written.

CHAPTER 2

This chapter gives us a good picture of how Holden sees himself, especially in relation to the adult world. In talking with his history teacher, Mr. Spencer, Holden constantly swings back and forth between what Spencer wants to hear and what he himself feels to be true.

He gives us a short sketch of Spencer as a man he thinks is too old to still be living, much less teaching. But then he admits that even people as old as the Spencers can enjoy things as simple as buying an authentic Navajo blanket.

NOTE: This sudden reversal illustrates another of Holden's interesting characteristics—his need to look at both sides of a question, even when he seems to have a strong opinion favoring one side. This trait keeps him from totally disliking anyone, because as soon as be becomes angry at someone, he thinks of the person's human side and tempers his opinion. The same characteristic keeps him from deciding many things about himself.

Holden has come to the home of his history teacher, who is sick in bed, even though he knew in advance that he wouldn't enjoy the visit. Still, he wasn't prepared for just how depressing the scene would be, and he regrets coming as soon as he walks into Spencer's bedroom. Throughout the visit Holden is uncomfortable and eager to leave.

As he talks with his teacher, Holden often mimics both the speech and the sentiments of adults. When he says he hasn't "communicated" with his parents, for example, he uses a word from Spencer's question, not from his everyday vocabulary. He does this often when he's talking with adults, not to impress them, but to hide his feelings of inferiority.

When he mimics adult sentiments, however, he uses them as a protective shield for his real feelings. Read what he says about Dr. Thurmer's comment that life is a game; then read how he really feels about that comment.

Why does Holden pretend to agree that life is a game when he feels so strongly that it isn't? Is it because he wants Mr. Spencer to think he's not such a "bad kid" after all? Or does he want to avoid arguing with Spencer (and with Thurmer) for some reason? As you learn more about Holden, you'll begin to form an opinion on that question and others like it. At this point it may be too early for you to tell.

Although Holden doesn't believe that life is a game, he does hold himself responsible for not measuring up like everyone else he knows. He berates himself for having "a lousy vocabulary," for acting young for his age, and for displeasing teachers like Spencer. He goes his own way often enough to have been expelled from four schools, but something inside him keeps telling him that he should be doing what other people do. You'll want to keep this personality conflict in mind as you read.

NOTE: In this chapter Holden picks up on something he mentioned only briefly before, a topic he'll return to again and again. The topic is phonies.

He told us in the first chapter that Pencey Prep's ad campaign was a phony, "strictly for the birds." Early in this chapter he's caught short by the word grand, a word he says he hates because it's a phony.

When Spencer mentions one of Holden's earlier schools, he decides not to try to explain his trouble there to Spencer because it "wasn't up his alley at all." He was "surrounded by phonies" at that school, Holden tells us, and his teacher wouldn't understand what he meant by that.

Even the headmaster was a phony there because he wouldn't spend much time with "little old funny-looking parents" on visiting day. Holden calls people phony because they are less perfect than he wants them to be. He is also at an age where it is easier to judge people than to try to understand them.

Holden's urge to protect the weak and vulnerable leads him to wonder (while he's giving Spencer "the old bull" about what a terrible student he is) about the ducks on the pond in Central Park in New York City. What happens to those ducks when the pond freezes during the winter? Does someone take care of them, or do they fly to a warmer climate? Like all sensitive adolescents, Holden has come to recognize the existence of sorrow and suffering in the world, and refuses to accept its inevitability.

CHAPTER 3

Going into his dormitory after leaving Mr. Spencer gives Holden another opportunity to expose the phoniness he sees all around him. This time he talks about a Pencey graduate named Ossenburger, for whom

Holden's dorm is named. Holden is more amused than angered by Ossenburger. In fact, you'll find that most of his descriptions of the phonies he hates are filled more with wisecracks than with angry statements.

He reaches his room and settles down to read a well-known serious book, *Out of Africa*, about life in East Africa. Mention of the book gives him the opportunity to knock himself once again, this time with a sentence that contradicts itself: "I'm quite illiterate, but I read a lot."

The contradiction underlines Holden's problem with his self-image. Someone who reads a lot can't be illiterate, by definition. But Holden is using the word to express other people's standards. What he means is, "I don't read what they want me to read, but I read a lot."

Here is the same personality conflict we saw in the last chapter. Holden knows what he wants to do, and he usually does it. That should make him feel good about himself. But adults keep telling him what they want him to do, and he can't shake the belief that not being able to please adults makes him a failure.

Holden comments that he would like to be able to talk on the telephone with authors of books he has enjoyed reading. This says something about how he personalizes things that happen to him, even something as impersonal as reading a book. This tendency is an important part of his makeup, and it becomes one of the causes of his illness later on.

Holden's solitary reading is interrupted by the entrance of Robert Ackley, a senior who lives in the next room. Ackley is a social "loser," not very pleasant looking, not very clean, and "sort of a nasty guy." (One of his problems is pimples. Does Salinger deliberately give him a name that sounds like "acne"? Probably not; most of the other characters have names that don't seem to signify anything.) Ackley is universally disliked, so it's no surprise that he, like Holden, is not at the game. (Holden would probably argue that he was alone by choice, but that a social misfit like Ackley was alone by necessity.)

One of Ackley's less endearing characteristics is his intrusiveness; once he's in Holden's room, he isn't about to leave. Their conversation is a comical collage of sarcastic (though not particularly witty) remarks, tough-guy cover-ups for feelings of insecurity, and horsing around, at least on Holden's part. In other words, it's a faithful re-creation of thousands of conversations that take place between teenage boys every day.

By now you should have developed some respect for Salinger's ability to capture the sounds of real speech. Because the story is told in the first person, every sentence in the book shows evidence of that ability. But when he deals with dialogue, as in this chapter, Salinger's job becomes a little more difficult because he has to capture the sounds of more than one person at a time. If you read the dialogue aloud you'll discover that none of the other characters in the book talks the way Holden does.

NOTE: Every once in a while something will remind you that the action is taking place not now, but around 1950. In his talk with Ackley, for instance, Holden sarcastically tells Ackley what a good sense of humor he has and offers to get him "on the goddamn radio." The reference to radio instead of television might jolt you a bit, just as you might have been surprised on the first page when Holden brags that his brother has a Jaguar that cost him "damn near four thousand bucks."

CHAPTER 4

In Chapter 3 Holden told us about someone he doesn't like—Ackley—who intruded on his privacy and generally made a nuisance of himself. Holden's feelings are easy to understand, because Ackley doesn't do much to endear himself to anyone.

In this chapter Holden talks with his roommate, Ward Stradlater. He agrees to write a descriptive composition for Stradlater. Though Stradlater isn't exactly a friend, he is someone Holden gets along with. Even so, Holden finds it as easy to criticize Stradlater as he does Ackley.

Although Holden talks about Stradlater in a friendlier way than he talked about Ackley, he criticizes Stradlater's whistling and his shaving habits. He admits that his roommate is handsome, but then withdraws the compliment by criticizing the *kind* of handsomeness he has. He brands Stradlater as insensitive and even adds that "he was a little bit like Ackley."

NOTE: Although the conversation he has with Stradlater is very different from the one he had with Ackley, Holden's criticisms sound very much alike to us. As you read, you'll find that Holden has trouble talking about almost anyone without being critical. This should set off a warning signal. If he complains so much about people, how valid can his complaints be? There's a possibility that the problem is with Holden, not with the people he knows.

Actually Holden doesn't complain about everyone. He has completely positive feelings about three people. He'll tell you about one, Jane Gallagher, in this chapter. In Chapter 5 you'll learn about a second one. The third person will enter the story later on.

While Holden is watching Stradlater shave in the bathroom, he does a spoof of a kind of musical movie that was popular during the 1930s and 1940s. He pretends to be the governor's son, who wants to become a tap dancer, against his father's wishes.

While he's telling us about it, he says, "I hate the movies like poison, but I get a bang imitating them." This might remind you of how he characterized his brother, D.B., in the first chapter. "Now he's out in Hollywood . . . being a prostitute."

NOTE: Holden will criticize movies a great deal throughout the book, but you'll find that he sees enough of them to qualify as a fan. His attitude toward movies (like his attitude toward many other things) is a mixture of acceptance and rejection. Something about movies makes him want to dislike them, but he seems to be drawn to them in spite of what he believes. Watch for other examples of this double-edged attitude, not only toward movies, but toward people and institutions.

Stradlater says that because of a change in plans he's dating a girl who knows Holden. When Holden finds out it's Jane Gallagher, he becomes flustered and begins babbling about the summer he spent living near her. (When he asks about "B.M." Holden wants to know if Jane attends Bryn Mawr, a noted college in Pennsylvania.)

With Stradlater ignoring him, Holden talks at length about Jane, catching his roommate's attention only when he mentions something that seems to suggest sex. "Only very sexy stuff interested him," Holden explains.

What interests Holden most about Jane, however, is something she used to do when they played checkers that summer. She'd put all her kings in the back row and leave them there because they looked so pretty.

Stradlater finds this boring. But Holden brings it up again just before his roommate leaves. Although he doesn't tell us why, Holden seems to think there's something vitally important in this quirk of Jane Gallagher's. It's likely that the quirk has a good deal to do with his fond memories of that summer, but we don't know yet for certain. In any case, Jane seems to be one of the vulnerable people in Holden's mind, and he tries to say something to that effect to Stradlater, who ignores him. The result is that Holden is afraid that Stradlater's good looks and smooth manner will allow him to take advantage of Jane. By the time Stradlater leaves, Holden is angry with him.

Thinking about the two of them on a date "made me so nervous I nearly went crazy," Holden tells us. He's so upset that he's glad to see Ackley barge back into his room.

CHAPTER 5

Holden decides to go into town to see a movie with another boy, Mal Brossard, and he asks Brossard if it would be all right to invite Ackley, "because Ackley never did *anything* on Saturday night, except stay in his room and squeeze his pimples or something." He tells us this without commenting on the irony of his wanting to invite someone he finds annoying, even disgusting.

NOTE: If you think about it briefly, you'll realize what a selfless gesture this is. And the fact that Holden doesn't comment on it suggests that the self-lessness comes naturally and doesn't even call for a comment.

The point is that Holden is beginning to reveal himself as a very good-hearted person. If you didn't see it in Chapter 1, when he said he liked Selma Thurmer in spite of the fact that she wasn't attractive or popular; if you didn't see it when he tried to keep Mr. Spencer from feeling bad about flunking him; if you didn't see it in the concern he expressed for Jane Gallagher, a girl he hasn't seen in nearly two years, then you should begin to see it now. In spite of what Holden would have us believe, he's a pretty good guy.

While he's waiting for Ackley to get ready for the movies, Holden opens a window and makes a snowball. His unwillingness to throw it comes from his appreciation for the untouched snow that looks "so nice and white." There's something in freshly fallen snow that affects everybody that way, but the clean perfection of the scene may have a special meaning for Holden. That perfection is related to innocence, which you'll find is very important to Holden. The really significant part of this chapter is the section about Allie, Holden's younger brother, who died three years earlier, when Holden was thirteen. Notice that the sentence, "He's dead now," comes almost as an afterthought to the description of Allie's glove that

Holden is writing as Stradlater's composition. By holding back this information, Holden signals us that he still has trouble accepting Allie's death.

Read the long paragraph about Allie very carefully. It's one of the most touching passages in the book because Holden is talking about a rarity in his life—someone he believes was truly good.

The passage about Allie is also important as a clue to why Holden is telling us this story from a hospital bed. Holden is still living with the trauma of his brother's death, a shock that has much to do with his current emotional state.

After the powerful section about Allie, Holden says of the baseball mitt, "I happened to have it with me, in my suitcase," and you recognize that he's once again trying to minimize something. You suspect that Holden probably hasn't gone anywhere without the glove since his brother died, a strong indication that Allie's death was a pivotal event in Holden's life.

It's probably the emotion of having talked and written about Allie that leads Holden to say something friendly at the end of the chapter. After listing everything that's wrong with Ackley, Holden says he feels sorry for this annoying character.

CHAPTER 6

"Some things are hard to remember," Holden says at the beginning of this chapter. By itself, this is a simple enough observation, but as you continue to read you'll find Holden making similar references to his loss of memory. If you keep in mind that he's telling his story from a hospital bed, and if you recall what he did when his brother Allie died and how he felt ("like I was sort of disappearing") when he ran to Mr. Spencer's house in the first chapter, you'll realize that something is not quite right with the way Holden sees himself and deals with the world. You can express what's wrong in a dozen different ways, and they may all be valid. Holden might still be trying to come to terms with Allie's death; he might be experiencing "emotional growing pains"; he might be on the verge of a serious breakdown. When you've finished the book, you can formulate your own statement (or statements) about Holden's problem with the world. For now, just collect all the important pieces of evidence as you find them.

When Stradlater comes back to change his clothes for a date, Holden gives him the composition. Stradlater's insensitive reaction to Holden's paper about Allie's baseball mitt is no great surprise. His teacher had told him to write a description of "a room or a house or something you once lived in," and it would never occur to someone like Stradlater that a description of a glove could also fulfill the assignment.

When he tells Holden, "You don't do *one damn thing* the way you're supposed to," Stradlater is touching on an important difference between him and his roommate. No matter what he does secretly, Stradlater is a person who follows the rules. ("It drove him crazy when you broke any rules.") He won't miss handing in an assignment, but he will get someone else to write it for him.

Stradlater is a "secret slob" who looks clean; what is true of his razor blade is also true of his behavior. Unlike Stradlater, Holden doesn't put up a front. He doesn't try very hard to please adults, and he's therefore known as someone who doesn't do anything the way he's supposed to.

After working himself into a frenzy over Jane Gallagher, Holden takes a swing at Stradlater, who promptly throws him to the floor and kneels on his chest. Nearly hysterical, Holden "told him he thought he could give the time to anybody he felt like. I told him he didn't even care if a girl kept all her kings in the back row or not."

In Holden's mind Jane Gallagher is so frail and vulnerable that she needs a solid line of kings to make her feel secure. In his mind Stradlater is a phony who uses his wiles to prey on frail and vulnerable girls.

Because he lives with Stradlater, there's a good chance that Holden is right about him. But how reliable is his evaluation of Jane Gallagher? She's a college student, older than he is; he hasn't seen her in two years; and she could very well have changed dramatically since he knew her.

None of this matters to Holden, of course. As far as he's concerned, One of the Helpless is out there, and it's his job to protect her. Or, as you'll find out later in the book, he would *like* that to be his job.

CHAPTER 7

After the fight with Stradlater, Holden goes next door and wakes up Ackley, hoping for some consolation but not really expecting any. (When he asks Ackley to play Canasta he's referring to a card game that was popular during the 1940s and 1950s.)

Holden has another bout of sarcastic bantering with Ackley. Then, since Ackley is Roman Catholic, Holden asks, "What's the routine on joining a monastery?"

The question leads to a funny exchange between the two, and then it's dropped. But don't let it slip by without thinking about it. If Holden were Catholic and devoted to his religion, thinking about a monastery might be a consistent thing for him to do. But joining a monastery has no religious meaning for

Holden; it would just be a way to escape the world that bothers him so much. It's true that many people have that kind of daydream from time to time. But as you get to know Holden, you'll find that it's more than a daydream, that the monastery is only one expression of a deep-seated desire to withdraw.

Holden decides not to wait until Wednesday, but to leave Pencey right then, late Saturday night, and to spend a few days alone in Manhattan before going home. He packs his bags, sells his typewriter to a boy down the hall, and leaves with a flourish, yelling *"Sleep tight, ya morons!"* on his way out.

NOTE: Remember that Holden has been through leave-taking scenes before. In the first chapter he told us he likes "to feel some kind of a good-by" when he leaves a place. He was able to think of something pleasant at that time, something that made him feel a little sorry to be leaving.

That isn't the case when he's actually on his way out the door, though. He's leaving abruptly, still angry at Stradlater, still annoyed with Ackley, and a bit uncomfortable that his exit isn't being acknowledged. His hostile good-bye yell may have made him feel better for the moment, but the leave-taking remains sour.

CHAPTER 8

As he's telling us about his walk to the train station, Holden mentions his "Gladstones," as he did when he packed to get ready to leave school. Notice how casually he drops the name of his expensive luggage, and think back to what he said about the Spencers not having a maid. The last thing Holden would want to do is impress you with his family's wealth. But these offhand references make it impossible to ignore how easily he takes money for granted.

It may not be a good idea to define someone by the amount of money he (or his family) has, but it would be foolish not to take it into account. With Holden (as with people in real life), you don't want to say, "He's a rich kid" and stop there. You do, however, want to say, "He's a rich kid with a certain attitude toward money and social position." Holden's attitude toward money is tied up with guilt. Watch for references to money as you read.

Holden's conversation during the train ride with Mrs. Morrow is funny. He thinks she's friendly and charming, even a bit sexually attractive. Since you don't know Holden very well this early in the story, you might think that he's a bit perverse in mentioning sex while describing a woman his mother's age.

But suspend your judgment for a while. Holden will talk with—and about—several girls and women before he's finished, and you'll have a more complete picture of his attitude toward the opposite sex. Then you can think back and evaluate this scene from a more informed vantage point.

In talking with Mrs. Morrow, Holden does something kind, then something a little cruel. The kind gesture is telling the woman what a gem she has for a son—Holden actually finds the boy to be nasty, but sees that Mrs. Morrow is worried about how her son is doing at school. Holden offers the kind gesture because he really likes the woman and because he tends to do kind things for people. (Remember, for example, how he tried to relieve Mr. Spencer of the pain caused by having to fail him.)

But then, to avoid telling her that he's been expelled from school, Holden invents a wild tale about having to go home for brain surgery. Mrs. Morrow is understandably upset by this news, and the only way Holden can avoid compounding the cruelty is to stop talking to her entirely.

The lie seems rather stupid because he was enjoying his conversation. You'll find that Holden does something like that in many situations. He seems to want to *stop* himself from succeeding at communicating with other people.

NOTE: Observe how Holden's language shifts in this chapter as he speaks with an adult. This shift is another indication of the good ear Salinger has for everyday language.

"He adapts himself very well to things," Holden says. And, "Some of the faculty are pretty conscientious." This is well-formulated, adult-type speech, quite different from the expletive-laden language he uses with other students. Back in Chapter 2, you heard Holden using similar language with Mr. Spencer.

CHAPTER 9

NOTE: When was the last time you told somebody something *really* personal? Try to remember what it felt like to reveal something you'd never told anyone before. Chances are you told less than the complete truth.

That's what most of us do when we're talking about very private matters, especially unpleasant ones. One side of you might want to tell the unvarnished truth. Another side, though, will try to put the best possible face on things, to make you look as good as possible.

Holden is just like anyone else in this regard, so you have to read between the lines to obtain a complete portrait of him. His narration is filled with comments that are phrased to sound casual, but reveal important things about him that he would probably hate putting into words.

The chapter opens with Holden telling us he "felt like giving somebody a buzz" when he reached Penn Station in New York City. That sounds casual enough to be ignored. But think about it for a moment.

He has just left the dorm, his temporary home, and he's arrived in the city of his permanent home, the city in which he plans to live like an adult for a few days before going home. It's late at night, and he's standing nearly alone in a huge railroad station.

He has no immediate plan in mind. He has nowhere to go. He has nobody to talk to. He's so much in need of a human connection that he'd settle for just about anyone he knows. He wants to call *somebody*.

Holden is a lonely boy, but he can't bring himself to say it—to us or to himself. So he slips the information to us in a way that makes it sound as though he just feels like talking.

A couple of sentences later Holden mentions his younger sister Phoebe for the first time. You'll find out later that Phoebe is the most important person in his life. You'd never be able to tell it from this reference, though. Holden isn't ready to tell us about Phoebe yet, so he just glides past her in his list of people he considered calling.

When Holden takes a cab, we learn that he lives near Central Park, an expensive Manhattan neighborhood. During his conversation with the driver, he asks about the ducks in Central Park. He mentioned this subject in Chapter 2, when he was talking with Mr. Spencer, and his concern with those ducks is an important clue to his personality, another indication of his concern for vulnerable creatures.

NOTE: During the cab ride scene, Holden uses the word "corny" to mean something like "fake" or "artificial." A page or two later he uses "crumby" to mean "sexual."

His use of "corny" seems to be due to his inability—or unwillingness—to think of the right word. But his use of "crumby" may be more important. He's talking about sex in that paragraph, and he becomes almost explicit. But he keeps using the almost meaningless word "crumby" instead of "sexual" or one of its synonyms. Think about "crumby" and its connotations, and you'll have some idea of Holden's dislike—possibly fear—of the implications of a sexual relationship.

The rest of the chapter shows Holden telephoning from the hotel room, trying unsuccessfully to arrange a date with a woman whose name he got from a college student. The scene is both touching and comical, and it could stand as an illustration of the ambivalence he's already expressed about sex, because he does a lot to talk himself *out of* the date he's supposedly trying to get.

CHAPTER 10

NOTE: Think about Holden's loneliness and how it affects everything he does. When he arrived in the city, he told us he wanted to call somebody—anybody, really. But he came up with a different reason for not calling each person he thought of. He ended up calling someone he'd never met, and pretending he was someone he wasn't.

Earlier we saw him try to explain to Mr. Spencer why he was being expelled. He soon realized that he and Spencer were talking different languages, and he hurried to get out of his teacher's house.

His conversations with Ackley were disastrous. The first time they talked, Ackley forced himself on Holden. But the second time, Holden did the forcing because he was desperate for someone to talk to.

On the train he met a woman he really liked. How did he deal with that potentially pleasant situation? He gave her a false name, drew a fraudulent picture of her son, and told her an outrageous lie about himself that effectively ended their conversation.

If there's a pattern here, it is that Holden wants to connect with people but can't, even when he has good opportunities. Though he tries talking to people, they all disappoint him, and he withdraws from them before anything can happen.

So far Holden has mentioned only two people for whom he has a continuing regard. One is Jane Gallagher, a girl he hasn't seen in almost two years. The other is his brother Allie, who has been dead for three years. Neither of these people is a part of Holden's life. For all we know, what he believes about them might be the product of his imagination.

At the beginning of Chapter 10 you'll read about a third person in this select group of people Holden thinks highly of. This one is alive, a part of his life, and very real. It's his younger sister Phoebe, and you'll meet her later in the story.

Read the opening of Chapter 10 with a pencil in your hand, because Holden (Salinger, actually) really gets carried away talking about Phoebe, and you might want to mark off some of the things he says about her. She's pretty, she's smart, she looks like Allie, she's "roller-skate skinny," and so on.

Phoebe is about the age Allie was when he died. Keep this in mind as you read the passage and as you continue to read the book. It will eventually give you a key to understanding Holden—and it is closely related to the book's title.

The passage about Phoebe contains something else of interest—some detailed references to movies. Holden has already told us several times how much he dislikes movies. The most memorable remark he made was at the end of the opening paragraph of the book, when he called his brother a prostitute for working in Hollywood.

On the other hand, he makes many references to movies, some of them rather affectionate, such as the one in this section about *The 39 Steps*. His attitude toward movies is at least ambivalent; he certainly doesn't hate them as much as he would have us believe.

NOTE: Why does Holden protest about movies so much, when he obviously sees many of them? It might be that Holden (who reads much more than his teachers think he does) feels movies should be beneath him. It might be that he has to convince himself from time to time that he really is an outsider.

What better way to do that than to divorce himself from the most popular form of entertainment of his time? Or his complaints about movies might be an indirect echo of his dissatisfaction with his brother D.B., who gave up writing the stories Holden loves in order to become a screenwriter.

Holden tells us he goes down to the hotel bar "to see what was going on." But by this time you should be suspicious of such casual language. In fact, he's still in the state he was in when he arrived at Penn Station, and when he called a total stranger. What he's longing for is to make contact with another person.

Does he have a chance of making contact? He spots three women, older than he is, but probably wanting as much as he does to meet someone. "The whole three of them were pretty ugly," he says, and he doesn't think much of the way they're dressed, either. He refers to them as "the three witches," and he works up a good deal of hostility toward them before he even approaches them.

How good, then, do you think his chances are of striking up a friendly conversation with these women? If he fails to connect—and of course he does—is it because they're insensitive dolts? If so, is it *only* because of that? Or does Holden play some part in these dead-end conversations he keeps finding himself in? Notice how often he finds the *wrong* thing to say to people. Notice how adept he is at appearing hostile, even though we know he's desperate to make contact. If Holden can't find someone to talk with, it's often as much his fault as that of the people he meets.

By the time the three women walk out on him, Holden has the explanation for his failure all prepared. "They were so ignorant, and they had those sad, fancy hats on and all. And that business about getting up early to see the first show at Radio City Music Hall depressed me."

It makes him so depressed he can't stand it, he tells us. He's already used the word "depressed" a few times, and he'll use it many more times later on. Pay attention to the kinds of things he finds depressing. The pattern will help you understand Holden better.

CHAPTER 11

Because Jane Gallagher is one of the three people Holden has had good things to say about, it pays to read this chapter carefully. Mull over some of the things he says about Jane. Try reading what he *means*, instead of only what he *says*. (Remember, sometimes even *he* doesn't know what his words reveal about himself, so this kind of reading isn't easy.)

Holden spends the whole chapter talking about Jane. He becomes so depressed thinking of her date with Stradlater that he ends up going to a bar.

"I know old Jane like a book," Holden tells us. How are we to take that? He hasn't seen her in nearly two years, since she was sixteen. He has missed a very important stage of her development as a young woman. The girl who went out with Stradlater may be radically different from the Jane who exists in Holden's memory. (Would the old Jane have gone near someone like Stradlater?)

"You don't always have to get too sexy to get to know a girl," he says. This tells us that his relationship with Jane was platonic—friendly but nonsexual. It also helps us understand why Holden would be upset that anyone could think of Jane in sexual terms.

When Holden says, "The girls I like best are the ones I never feel much like kidding . . . it's hard to get started, once you've known them a pretty long time and never kidded them," he's suggesting that he's in awe of girls, that he can't treat them casually as friends.

When he thinks about Jane and Stradlater in Ed Banky's car, it drives him crazy, even though "I knew she wouldn't let him get to first base with her." It drives him crazy because he doesn't truly know what Jane would allow Stradlater to do. He's frightened by the possibility that Jane might have changed.

Remember, Jane is the only person outside of his family to whom Holden has ever shown Allie's glove. Allie and Phoebe represent childhood innocence to Holden. If he has linked them with Jane in his mind, her growing up could be a terrible event in his life.

CHAPTER 12

Early in this chapter, Holden says, "New York's terrible when somebody laughs on the street very late at night. . . . It makes you feel so lonesome and depressed."

There's that word "depressed" again. You'll see it a few more times in this chapter, and you'll notice it cropping up more and more often as Holden goes on with his story. Loneliness—the inability to make contact with people—is one part of Holden's problem. Almost constant depression is another part.

NOTE: What makes Holden sad? It might be better to ask what *doesn't* make him sad. He seems to find something depressing in almost everything and everyone he meets. After a while, you begin to see that the problem is much more internal than anything else—that Holden's depression comes from the way he sees things, not necessarily from the way they are.

On his way to Ernie's bar, Holden has a long conversation with a cab driver about those Central Park ducks. The cab driver is a funny character, so the scene is enjoyable to read. But don't forget that those ducks are important to Holden; they'll become even more important as the story progresses.

As he did with the first cab driver, Holden asks this one to join him for a drink. Later he sends a message to the piano player to ask if he'll join him for a drink. Try to imagine how desperate he is to have someone to talk to. Imagine how lost and alone you'd have to feel to ask strangers to spend some time with you. And keep in mind that Holden doesn't seem to realize what these desperate requests signify about himself.

When you read Holden's comments about the people at the bar, watch for the pendulum swings in his attitude. For example, he hates the way Ernie is playing the piano, but "I felt sort of sorry for him when he was finished." He makes fun of the people sitting on his left, but ends by saying, "Real ugly girls have it tough. I feel so sorry for them sometimes." He doesn't like anything about Lillian Simmons, but "You had to feel sort of sorry for her, in a way."

His feeling sorry for people, feeling sad, and becoming depressed all seem to be snowballing. The references are coming closer together; they're playing a larger part in his story. Something is happening to Holden.

"I was surrounded by jerks," he says at one point in this chapter. This statement could fit comfortably into almost every chapter you've read so far. To Holden, just about everybody is a jerk. He does feel sorry for most jerks, instead of feeling superior to them. But they're jerks just the same.

The chapter ends with the statement, "People are always ruining things for you." This encapsulates Holden's troubles with the world.

CHAPTERS 13 AND 14

Holden's red hunting hat reappears at the beginning of Chapter 13. He bought the hat right after he lost the fencing equipment on his trip with the team. Some critics have suggested that the hat symbolizes Holden's alienation from the world in which he lives. Holden bought it, after all, when the team members "ostracized" him, and it does set him apart from everyone else.

If you don't feel comfortable with symbolism, you can think of the hat as a sign of Holden's eccentricity, a poster that announces, "I'm not like the rest of you." It isn't of major importance, but even minor things should be considered when you're analyzing a character as complex as Holden.

As he's walking the forty-one blocks from Ernie's bar to the hotel, Holden misses his gloves, which he thinks were stolen at school. He thinks about what he might have done if he'd caught the thief, and this leads him to say, "I'm one of these very yellow guys." By "yellow," Holden means he doesn't like fighting. In fact he might take any route to avoid it.

His imaginary dialogue with the thief who stole his gloves is rather funny. In his mind he begins by accusing the thief, then tempering the accusation, then backing off, then leaving the room to go to the bathroom and look tough in the mirror. Most people find the imaginary dialogue funny because most people are as reluctant to fight as Holden is.

Holden, however, has an excuse for not fighting in a situation like the one he's described: "I never seem to have anything that if I lost it I'd care too much," he says, meaning that none of his possessions seems important enough to justify fighting. Still, he doesn't let himself off that easily. He's ashamed of not being willing to fight. "What you should be," he says, "is not yellow at all."

He adds that he hates fights because he's more afraid of hurting someone than of being hurt. But even that isn't an acceptable excuse. It's just "a funny kind of yellowness."

Holden is torn between two standards of behavior—the traditional "macho" standard and the gentle one that comes more naturally to him. His weak self-image won't allow him to entertain the idea that his own standard of behavior is preferable.

Thinking about yellowness depresses him. He reaches his hotel and walks inside. The lobby depresses him, so he enters the elevator. When the elevator operator offers to get a woman for him, he accepts because he's so depressed.

While he's waiting for the prostitute to come to his room, Holden thinks about sex, a subject he has already told us confuses him a great deal. Like his thoughts on cowardice, much of what he says about sex will sound very, very familiar—and therefore probably funny.

When he was talking about being "yellow," Holden said he was afraid of hurting someone in a fight. Here he says he doesn't want to take advantage of girls. Girls in general seem to fit into Holden's classification of vulnerable people, and that, of course, complicates his feelings about sex.

By the time Sunny, the prostitute, reaches his room, Holden is a nervous wreck. He works hard at appearing urbane, but Sunny seems hardly aware of him. In no time at all he's feeling sorry for her, and he tells her he isn't in the mood for sex. She asks for double the price mentioned by the elevator operator, but he refuses to give her more than he agreed to.

The time he spends with the prostitute depresses him further. It also has another effect on him, one that he can describe only as "peculiar." That's an odd word for Holden to use, and, in fact, it signals that something is happening to him. Think of his memory blackouts. Think of the time he felt that he was disappearing. Then look at what he does after Sunny leaves.

He sits down and starts talking to Allie, his dead brother. "I do that sometimes when I get very depressed," he tells us. He talks about something he did to Allie once, something that makes him feel guilty when he thinks about it. And he tells us he thinks about it when he gets depressed.

The part about Allie is followed by Holden's thoughts on Jesus and the Disciples. (The Disciples, or Apostles, were twelve men whom Jesus chose to help him preach his new doctrines. What Holden refers to as "the Bible" is actually the *New Testament*, which describes the life and teachings of Jesus.)

Holden loves Jesus, but he has little use for the Disciples. Jesus taught that people should love one another without qualifications. Holden believes that Jesus meant that literally, and lived up to it. The Disciples, however, were ordinary men who had difficulty carrying out Jesus' teachings to the letter. Holden doesn't have much patience with them, and that should tell you how high—how impossible—a standard he uses to measure people.

The elevator operator returns with Sunny and demands another five dollars. Holden stands up to him, but it's clear from the beginning that they'll get the money out of him. In his anger, Holden insults the elevator operator, who punches him in the stomach.

Then Holden treats us to another of his affectionate movie tributes. He ends it, as always, by criticizing the movies, but by this time we should have learned to stop paying attention to his criticisms. The movie scenario is his way of turning a frightening, painful, and humiliating situation into a near-heroic one.

It's now Sunday morning, and we've been with Holden for less than twenty-four hours.

CHAPTER 15

Holden is still alone and still lonely. For the third time he thinks of calling Jane Gallagher and decides not to. "I wasn't in the mood," is the reason he gives to himself.

Maybe you can think of one or more explanations that come closer to the truth. Why would he keep hesitating to call her, when she's one of the few bright lights in his depressing world? What is he afraid might happen? What might he find when he talks to her?

Holden is trying to avoid having to face something about Jane that he finds threatening. He knows very well that Jane has grown up since he knew her. If she were still the same girl, it's unlikely that she would have gone on a date with Stradlater. If he calls her, he'll have to face the real Jane, not the innocent girl he once knew. And he isn't ready for the real Jane.

So he calls Sally Hayes instead. She's a beautiful girl, but a phony, at least by Holden's standards. He arranges to take her to a play that afternoon, and he quickly leaves the hotel. He takes a cab to Grand Central Station, where he leaves his suitcases in a rented locker.

Then he goes to a coffee shop, where he sees two nuns having trouble with their suitcases. He helps them and has a very unusual experience—a pleasant conversation with someone he genuinely likes.

Notice that even though this is an upbeat scene, Holden is depressed. He feels badly about the nuns' inexpensive suitcases and about the meager meal they're having.

He says several times that he doesn't like having things that are better than other people's. While he seems to take his father's wealth for granted, something about having money bothers him. The last thing he says in this chapter is a good summary of his attitude: "Goddam money," he says. "It always ends up making you feel blue as hell."

NOTE: When Holden thinks that someone is vulnerable, he wants to shield him or her from sorrow and pain. Rather than compromise with life and accept the existence of suffering, he dreams of making the world over in his own youthful image. He is too young to accept the fact that there are things in life he cannot control. In this chapter, Holden is afraid of being too specific about *Romeo and Juliet* because it concerns a love affair, and the nuns might be embarrassed. He considers these nuns vulnerable, in need of protection. Of course, he's wrong about that. They're grown women, college graduates, professional teachers. But he sees them as creatures who have to be protected from the realities of the world.

That's the way he felt about Jane Gallagher when he fought with Stradlater. He was probably just as wrong about her needing his protection, but that doesn't matter. When Holden perceives someone as vulnerable, he wants to shield him or her from the world.

CHAPTER 16

This is one of the most important chapters in the book because Holden comes very close to verbalizing what's been bothering him. (Remember, he hasn't been holding back. He just doesn't know what's bothering him.)

He has some final thoughts about the nuns, which he sums up in a curious way: "That's what I liked about those nuns. You could tell, for one thing, that they never went anywhere swanky for lunch. It made me so damn sad when I thought about it, their never going anywhere swanky for lunch or anything."

Think about that for a minute. What he likes about them is the same thing that makes him sad. That isn't exactly a self-contradiction, but it *is* strange. And it's a clue to why Holden is so troubled. Even the positive things he encounters are tainted in some way. He's unable to enjoy anything because nothing is perfect. The result is that even good things make him sad.

What he likes about certain people should make him happy. Why doesn't it? Because the world doesn't value the things he values. There's a gap—sometimes a huge one—between the beautiful world inside Holden's head and the ugly one outside him. And Holden isn't having much luck bridging that gap.

The rest of the chapter is almost exclusively about children, and that's what makes it very important. You know that Holden has an idealized picture of the world in his mind, but where does that picture come from? In this chapter you'll learn that it comes from his ideas about childhood.

While he's walking the streets, killing time until his date with Sally, Holden comes across a six-year-old boy walking with his parents. The boy is singing the Scottish folk song "Comin' Through the Rye," but he doesn't have the lyrics quite right. The lyrics actually are, "If a body *meet* a body. . . ." The boy is singing, "If a body *catch* a body comin' through the rye." (Later, the boy's mistake will appear in the significance of the book's title.)

"It made me feel better," Holden says. "It made me feel not so depressed any more." Just the sight of a child enjoying himself in his own little world, totally oblivious to everything around him, is enough to overcome what seems to be constant sadness in Holden. Without doing anything special, the boy lifts Holden out of his depression. This is your first clue about how important children are to him.

After buying Phoebe a record on Broadway, Holden walks uptown to Central Park, where he hopes to find his sister skating. When he reaches the park, he has another of those strange symptoms that seem to be indications of a serious physical or mental illness.

He's talking about the park when he says, "It made you depressed, and every once in a while, for no reason, you got goose flesh when you walked." The gooseflesh is like his dizziness or the feeling that he's about to disappear. These symptoms appear with no warning, but he talks about them casually, as though they happen to everybody. He stops and talks to a girl who knows Phoebe. She tells him Phoebe is probably at the American Museum of Natural History, and Holden helps her tighten her skates. Helping her and being thanked make him nearly ecstatic.

When the girl leaves, he begins walking to the museum, where he used to go regularly when he was Phoebe's age. On the way there, he gives us a detailed description of the museum's lifelike statues and dioramas, and we begin to get a picture of how much Holden loved his childhood.

NOTE: The museum represents Holden's childhood to him. "I loved that damn museum," he tells us. One of the things he means is that he loved the way the world was (or seemed, at least) when he was a child.

"The best thing, though, in that museum was that everything always stayed right where it was," he explains. And in the next paragraph he adds, "Certain things they should stay the way they are. You ought to be able to stick them in one of those big glass cases and just leave them alone."

Holden is close to revealing—to himself as well as to us—just what's wrong with his life. His next sentence is, "I know that's impossible." But does he *really* know that?

If he knows it's impossible to preserve things as they were in childhood, why does he talk to Allie in moments of stress? Why is his ten-year-old sister one of the few people he admires? Why does he continue to think of Jane as a frail creature who keeps her kings in the back row, when she's matured enough to date someone like Stradlater?

He remembers his own experience of being different each time he went to the museum, though everything there remained exactly as it had been before. He thinks about Phoebe being different every time she goes. "It didn't exactly depress me to think about it," he says, "but it didn't make me feel gay as hell, either."

Those changes he remembers were signs that his life had progressed, that he had grown up little by little. He knows the same thing will happen to Phoebe, but he doesn't like thinking about it.

Just before he reaches the museum, Holden offers a helping hand to two small children on a seesaw, although "you could tell they didn't want me around, so I let them alone." That may be the saddest event in this chapter, but Holden doesn't comment on it.

He seems to be overflowing with good feelings for small children, much as a parent would be for his or her own children. But he also shares something else with parents: the knowledge that they can't do everything they'd like to do for their children, that they have to let them do as much as possible by themselves. Holden may be unconscious of this knowledge, but it's what keeps him from helping the children, no matter how much he'd like to.

When he reaches the museum he has so lovingly described, he decides not to go inside. He probably knows it won't be as beautiful as he remembers it. After all, if Jane Gallagher can grow up, what's to prevent the museum from changing?

CHAPTER 17

Holden's references to sadness and depression, coupled with his mental trip back to the beauty of childhood, are signals that the tension in him is mounting. It's becoming more difficult for him to cope as the hours pass. In this chapter he almost forces a crisis.

He's waiting for Sally in the lobby of New York's Biltmore Hotel, a popular meeting place for young people at the time that Salinger was writing. The place is filled with girls his age, and he's watching them. It was "nice sightseeing," he says, but also "sort of depressing."

The depressing part is thinking about what's going to happen to most of the girls he sees. They're all going to have conventional lives, he thinks, married to boring men. But notice where Holden's thoughts about bores lead him. He ends up saying that life with a bore might not be so bad after all. Even a bore, he thinks, has at least one quality that sets him above everyone else, or one special talent that no one else has.

His date with Sally resembles an emotional roller coaster ride. "I felt like marrying her the minute I saw her," he says. On the way to the theater, he tells her he loves her. Though he knows it's a lie, he says he meant it when he said it. By the time they leave the theater, he "sort of hated old Sally."

"I'm crazy," he tells us. Later, he calls himself a madman. Of course, he means these statements as figures of speech, but they still indicate that he has some idea that he's behaving erratically.

Sally suggests that they go ice skating. In a restaurant at the rink, Holden's troubles begin coming to a head. He tells Sally how much he hates school, and uncharacteristically he's willing to see himself, and not the rest of the world, as the problem.

"I don't get hardly anything out of anything," he cries. "I'm in bad shape. I'm in *lousy* shape." Unlike his use of "crazy" and "madman" earlier, this is no figure of speech for Holden. He's serious, he's admitting he's in trouble, and he's asking Sally to help him.

That, of course, is one of the most irrational things we've seen him do yet. Sally Hayes is the last person who might be willing to help him. She doesn't even understand most of what he's saying to her.

He makes the further mistake of asking her to come live in the woods with him. Her response would be funny if Holden's condition weren't so serious. As he has done all along, he's trying to reach out to someone. But, as usual, he's saying the wrong thing to the wrong person. The net result of Holden's attempt is that he annoys Sally by his use of profanity, and finally insults her.

NOTE: Once again, Holden's attempt at communication comes to nothing. Worse than nothing, really, because he's just alienated someone he's known for a long time. He does try to apologize, but Sally won't accept it, and she tells him he's mad.

So he's alone again, more depressed than ever, and angry with himself for asking Sally to go away with him.

"The terrible part, though," he says, "is that I *meant* it when I asked her." And that really is terrible, because it shows that Holden has nearly lost control of himself.

Sally Hayes isn't someone with whom Holden wants to live. He can't even endure an afternoon with her. His invitation to her is the irrational act of a desperate person, someone who will do anything for human companionship.

CHAPTERS 18 AND 19

Now that his date is over, Holden starts thinking about girls again. "The trouble with girls," Holden says, "is, if they like a boy, no matter how big a bastard he is, they'll say he has an inferiority complex, and if they *don't* like him, no matter how nice a guy he is, or how big an inferiority complex he has, they'll say he's conceited. Even smart girls do it."

Even Jane Gallagher, the girl he has idealized in his mind, has been known to do it. What he's saying is that sexual attraction can make girls see things the way they want them to be, instead of the way they are.

He seems to forget, though, that he does the same thing himself. Near the beginning of Chapter 15, Holden told us that when he necks with a girl, he has to think she's intelligent, even if she isn't. He wants to believe he can have relationships only with girls he respects, but he puts his standards aside as readily as the girls about whom he's complaining.

He's alone again, and he wants to be with somebody. When he gets no answer at Jane Gallagher's number, he calls an older boy who used to be his adviser at the school he attended before Pencey. They agree to meet that night, and Holden has several hours to kill.

What does he do? He goes to Radio City Music Hall, showing himself once again to be a jumble of contradictions. How many times has he told us he hates movies? Remember how depressed he became when he heard the three women at the hotel bar talking about going to Radio City? You'd think he'd rather die than go into the place. And here he is spending several hours there.

Needless to say, he finds it all very depressing. He's especially upset by the religious spectacle commemorating Christmas—a yearly event for which Radio City is world famous. It leads, naturally enough, to some thoughts about Jesus, and that brings Allie to mind.

Notice how casually Holden can move from Jesus to Allie, and don't miss the importance of that. Allie is as much a religious figure to him as Jesus, maybe even more so. When Holden's condition worsens later on, you'll see him begin to pray to his dead brother.

After these thoughts about Radio City and religion, Holden starts talking about the movie. He gives a detailed summary of the plot, all the while telling us how much he hated it. "It was so putrid I couldn't take my eyes off it." But he was interested enough to have remembered every twist of the plot, no matter how trite it was.

The people in the audience at the theater upset him, as do the patrons at the bar where Ernie played the piano. His comments now are beginning to sound repetitious. He says the same thing at Radio City that he said at Ernie's and at the play he saw with Sally. He becomes upset at these performances because he thinks people are applauding the grandstanding and showing off, not the talent. He becomes even more upset at the possibility that the performers themselves no longer know the difference between showing off and creating something beautiful. (See the Author's Life and Times for some thoughts on how this sentiment may reflect Salinger's attitude.)

After the movie, Holden walks to the bar where he is to meet Carl Luce, an older boy who used to be his adviser. Early in Chapter 18, he describes Luce as "one of those very intellectual guys." Early in Chapter 19, Holden adds enough about him to suggest that

Luce may be a sex pervert. In any case, Luce always seemed preoccupied with sex, and sex is what Holden wants to talk to him about.

Luce, however, is now a college student, more discreet than he was a few years ago when he talked sex with the younger boys in the school. But Holden keeps pushing to get him to talk. As Sally did a few hours earlier, Luce tells Holden more than once to keep his voice down. Though Holden denied it in the afternoon, he admits now that he was "talking a little too loud." He may even be beginning to sound hysterical.

His tone and his insistence on talking about sex almost guarantee that this conversation will end as most of Holden's attempts at communication have. Luce cuts it short and leaves. But not before Holden begs him to stay awhile. "Please," he says. "I'm lonesome as hell. No kidding."

But Luce, like Sally, is a semistranger. He has little compassion for this boy he barely knows, and Holden has done very little in their few minutes together to earn any.

CHAPTERS 20 AND 21

Holden *is* repeating himself, going around in circles that are becoming smaller and smaller. At the beginning of Chapter 20, still in the bar and drinking heavily after Luce has left him, he asks a waiter to invite one of the female dancers to have a drink with him. The waiter says he'll deliver the message, but Holden doubts that he will. "People never give your message to anybody," he says.

Compare this to the scene at Ernie's in Chapter 12 when he told a waiter to invite Ernie to his table for a drink. His comment on that waiter was almost exactly the same.

Holden gets so drunk that he has to dunk his head in a sink filled with cold water. He goes out and starts walking uptown toward the lake in Central Park. Outside in the cold air, the water begins to freeze in his hair, and he starts thinking about catching pneumonia and dying.

He talks about this in the same offhand tone he uses for everything, so it would be easy to miss its significance. Review his situation for a minute. He's drunk; he has no money left; he's freezing; he's been thrown out of school; he can't go home; he has no other friends to call; he's desperate for someone to talk to; he's even more desperate for someone to tell him what to do; and he has no reason to think his situation will be better in the morning.

When he talks about dying, it isn't in the same way he pretended to have a bullet in his stomach, after the elevator operator had punched him in the hotel room. Dying would be a relief to him. It would solve all the problems he can't get a grip on. From his angle, getting pneumonia might be the best thing that's happened to him in a long time.

He has these thoughts, and the thoughts about Allie in the cemetery, while he's at the lake in Central Park. He's still curious about those ducks, which he finds are gone now that the lake is frozen.

Remember Holden's need to protect the vulnerable. His concern for the ducks is one expression of that need. He may have lost his perspective by giving the ducks more importance than they should have. But his concern comes from the same urge that makes him worry about Jane Gallagher and about Phoebe having to grow up.

Now you're finally about to meet Phoebe. Holden leaves the deserted lake, intent on sneaking into his apartment and talking with his sister. He describes his "breaking and entering" in a funny passage at the beginning of Chapter 21.

Pay special attention to everything he says about Phoebe. When he talks about her, Holden is *happy*. He becomes tender and avoids the wisecracks that usually fill his sentences. Everything he says sounds touching. He's telling you about the only living person he loves.

Not only does he love her, but she's also a child, and children are among the vulnerable people. As you saw in Chapter 16, children make Holden very happy. In this chapter he says, "I can read that kind of stuff, some kid's notebook . . . all day and all night long. Kid's notebooks kill me."

When he wakes Phoebe up and talks to her, you'll see why he loves her so. She's bright, articulate, and mature for her age, the kind of little sister any teenage boy would love to have.

NOTE: There are two things to note especially in Holden and Phoebe's conversation. First, Phoebe's announcement of the exciting news that they have a radio in the car is a detail that reminds you that the novel was written in the 1940s. Second, when Phoebe realizes why Holden is home three days early, she begins to sound like his older sister.

You'll see more of that in the next chapter.

CHAPTER 22

"She was ostracizing the hell out of me," Holden says. "Just like the fencing team at Pencey when I left all the goddam foils on the subway."

This reference brings you back to the very beginning of the story, the fifth paragraph of the novel, when he talked about the fencing foils. Maybe it's an indication that Holden has come full circle, that he hasn't accomplished anything, that he's right back where he started. There's another full-circle reference later in this chapter, when Holden says he's going to visit a former teacher of his. It's likely that Salinger is trying to direct our attention to the beginning of the story.

Phoebe talks to Holden "like a goddam schoolteacher," and he responds as he might to an older person, in a petulant and whining manner. When she asks him why he's being expelled again, he tries to explain what a terrible place Pencey is.

The trouble is, his description could fit any school, or almost any group situation that any of us will ever be in. Holden may think he's complaining about Pencey; in fact, he's complaining about the world.

Phoebe really becomes the adult character when she presses him to name something he really likes. She won't accept either of the answers he gives, and she presses the issue by asking him what he wants to be.

Holden's response contains the source of the book's title. He wants to be the catcher in the rye because he wants to prevent small children from getting hurt.

NOTE: His catcher in the rye image, far-fetched as it is, is the first concrete expression of Holden's urge to protect the vulnerable that we've been hearing about throughout the novel. It explains his feelings for Jane Gallagher (at least the Jane he knew during that summer vacation). It explains the concern he felt in the coffee shop for the nuns' sensibility, the feeling he has for girls in general, and the tenderness that overtakes him when he talks with or about children.

It explains why he likes Jesus, who preached love and sacrifice, even though he considers himself an atheist. It explains why he feels sorry for people who don't have the money or possessions he has, and why he sympathizes with social misfits like Ackley.

Holden just wants to prevent everyone from getting hurt. His image deals with children because no one is more vulnerable than they are. But his urge to protect extends to everyone.

Although this may sound beautiful, think of the negative side for a moment. Holden offered the catcher in the rye image in response to Phoebe's question about what he wanted to do with his life. This isn't a dream he's describing. He says it's "the only thing I'd really like to be."

Take that as a clue that Holden's grasp of reality isn't as firm as it should be. He doesn't imagine himself doing anything remotely attainable. He doesn't talk about entering teaching, social work, the clergy, medicine, or any other profession or occupation that would allow him to satisfy his urge to help people. He imagines himself only as the catcher in the rye.

As he admitted earlier in the day to Sally, he's in lousy shape.

CHAPTERS 23 AND 24

Holden's phone call to Mr. Antolini, "about the best teacher I ever had," brings us back to the beginning of the novel, when he visited Mr. Spencer before leaving Pencey. When you read about his visit with this teacher, contrast it with the visit he made in

Chapter 2. Antolini is an adult Holden wants to talk to, in the hope that he can get some helpful advice.

Before Holden can leave the apartment, his parents come home unexpectedly. He hides in the closet and listens as Phoebe deftly handles the questions her mother asks. The conversation between Phoebe and Mrs. Caulfield is interesting because Phoebe is completely in control, and her mother is being manipulated.

Mrs. Caulfield goes to bed, and Holden prepares to leave. Before he leaves he starts to cry, which upsets his sister very much. His crying seems to have been brought on by the appearance of his mother. Holden has told us before that he feels guilty about the trouble he causes her, and his guilt feelings have grown worse since Allie's death.

As he's trying to bring himself under control, he says, "I thought I was going to choke to death or something." This is the first in a series of physical symptoms that signal Holden's approaching breakdown.

He slips out of the house successfully, but he seems to be wearying of the freedom he anticipated when he left Pencey on Saturday night. At the end of Chapter 23 he says he almost wished his parents had caught him on the way out.

Mr. and Mrs. Antolini live on Sutton Place, one of the most expensive streets in Manhattan. Unlike Mr. Spencer, Mr. Antolini is young, sophisticated, rich, and witty. Holden comes to see him because he wants to, not because he thinks he should. He's hoping to get some help from Antolini, something he wouldn't dream of asking from Spencer.

He takes a cab to their house because he feels dizzy when he leaves his building. The dizziness is compounded by a severe headache; Holden's physical condition is deteriorating.

Read Chapter 24 carefully. The conversation summarizes much of what has been happening to Holden, and Antolini's advice, unlike Spencer's well-meaning clichés, is personalized and to the point. Antolini is genuinely concerned about Holden, so much so that he has recently met with Mr. Caulfield to discuss Holden s problems.

Because school is where most of Holden's problems are evident, school is what he talks about with his former teacher. Their conversation amounts to a discussion of educational philosophy, though Antolini is understandably more articulate than Holden on the subject.

Antolini warns him about people who destroy themselves by "looking for something their own environment couldn't supply them with." That's not a bad description of Holden's trouble. He seems to expect something from the world that the world can't deliver.

Antolini warns Holden about what might happen if he doesn't overcome this problem. He also explains how doing well in school could help someone in that situation, and how it could be particularly valuable to Holden. Education, he says, will help Holden learn that "you're not the first person who was ever confused and frightened and even sickened by human behavior."

Antolini's advice is right on the mark, and you could read this chapter with some optimism, some hope that maybe he can help Holden improve his situation. Then Antolini spoils it all by putting his hand on Holden's forehead and scaring the wits out of him.

NOTE: You can read the last section of the chapter a dozen times and never be absolutely sure if Antolini makes a pass at Holden. Some readers say that there's no doubt that he does and that Salinger has even prepared us for it.

"How're all your women?" Antolini asks Holden just before he goes to sleep on the couch. And the last thing he says to Holden is, "Good night, handsome." In addition, he and his wife never seem to be in the same room, there's a great difference in their ages, and their attraction for each other may not be sexual.

Other readers think Antolini never makes a pass at all. He's genuinely concerned with Holden's welfare, they say, and he knows what a fragile state Holden is in. Even if he were homosexual, he wouldn't put Holden's health in jeopardy because he's clearly a responsible teacher.

The question is, was Holden premature in assuming that Antolini was making a pass? There is no definite answer. You'll have to draw your own conclusion.

More important than that question is the effect the scene has on Holden. He's just been given some valuable advice by a man he respects. Now he has run out of the man's house in fear. The real problem is that he might run from the advice as well as from the man who gave it.

CHAPTER 25

In a sense, everything Holden counted on has been taken away from him. Phoebe didn't give him the understanding and compassion he was hoping for. She even wrenched Allie from him as a source of comfort by coldly reminding him that their dead brother is no longer real. He hasn't been able to get in touch with Jane Gallagher. And Mr. Antolini turned out to be the biggest disappointment of all.

Before this chapter is over Holden will have reclaimed some of what he's lost in the past few hours; whether that helps with his overall problem is something you'll have to decide when you've finished the book.

The first thing he reclaims, to a degree at least, is his regard for Antolini. When he wakes from a nap in Grand Central Station, he thinks about what happened at Antolini's, and he decides that he might have been wrong in thinking that the man was acting like a pervert. He has every reason to think of Antolini as a good person, and he could have misconstrued the situation.

Even after he's dealt with this question, though, Holden is still more alone than ever before, and his physical condition is deteriorating. His headache is worse, the dizziness continues, he can't swallow, and he's now troubled by nausea and diarrhea.

These are only his physical symptoms. They signal an even more serious emotional state, one we've been seeing signs of since Holden felt he was about to disappear on his way to Mr. Spencer's house.

While he's walking in Manhattan on this Monday morning, Holden sees things that point up both the ugliness and the beauty of the world he has so much trouble with. The ugliness is seen in the use of profanity by a man who's unloading a Christmas tree from a truck. It may be a hopeful sign that Holden finds this funny instead of depressing.

The beauty is seen in the Christmas shoppers who remind Holden of the fun he's had with Phoebe. As he walks up Fifth Avenue—once again toward Central Park—he's feeling rather cheerful because of those happy memories.

But not for long. He begins to feel that he's about to disappear, and he calls on Allie to keep it from happening. In spite of the trauma of hearing Phoebe remind him that Allie is dead, Holden is apparently intent on keeping his brother in his life. Finally, after walking a couple of miles, he sits on a park bench, perspiring and breathing heavily.

That's where he hatches his plan to escape all this trouble for good. The section begins in the middle of a long paragraph, with the sentence, "I decided I'd go away." Read it carefully—it's the other side of the catcher in the rye dream.

In this dream Holden would cut himself off from all human communication by running away and pretending to be a deaf mute. It's a more extreme version of an idea he mentioned to Ackley, when he asked about the possibility of a non-Catholic joining a monastery. Both schemes would allow him to disappear from the world, and on his own terms.

Because he wants to say good-bye to Phoebe, he goes to her school to have a note delivered to her in class. On his way to the principal's office he sees an obscenity scrawled on the wall, and it nearly destroys him. Small children are going to see this obscenity. It's going to disturb them and ruin the beauty of their childhood world. That makes Holden furious. As the catcher in the rye, he rubs the words out with his hand, intent on keeping the children from being hurt by the ugliness.

After he drops off the note for Phoebe, he leaves the principal's office and sees the same obscenity written on another wall. This one is scratched in, and even the catcher in the rye can't remove it to protect the children. Then he decides that it's a hopeless battle, anyway. You can't erase all the obscenities in the world.

NOTE: Is Holden admitting that ugliness is simply a fact of life? Is he *accepting* ugliness as something that can't be erased? Has he decided that he can't protect children from it, that he can't prevent them from growing up? Does he no longer want to be the catcher in the rye?

There are readers who say that the obscenity jolts Holden into an awareness of the real world that he didn't have before. And there are readers who say that he has only realized how monumental the problem is, without making any decision about giving up the battle. You'll have to see how Holden behaves in the few remaining pages of the book before you can say whether the obscenity has caused a major change in the way he looks at life.

While he's waiting for Phoebe to meet him at the museum, Holden talks with two children who are playing hooky from school and have come to see the Egyptian mummies. (This is the Metropolitan Museum of Art, not the American Museum of Natural History that Holden talked about earlier.) Look at the paragraph in which Holden explains to the boys how the Egyptians buried their dead. Then go back to Chapter 2 and reread the social studies essay answer that Mr. Spencer read aloud to Holden.

In the earlier version Holden was parroting textbook material for an essay question he found boring. Now he's using the same material, but because he's telling it to the boys, he's animated by the material and thinks it's "very interesting." Mr. Spencer probably wouldn't have appreciated the difference; Mr. Antolini certainly would have.

When the boys leave, Holden enjoys the peace and quiet in the tomb. But only for a moment, because he's slapped with another obscenity scrawled on the wall. This time he makes a joke about the obscenity. It's a bitter joke, but a joke all the same. The difference in his reaction may signal that something actually has happened to Holden.

There's also a difference in his deaf-mute daydream, which he talks about again on his way to meet Phoebe during her lunch hour. He has now expanded the daydream to include a trip back home when he's about thirty-five, and occasional visits from Phoebe and D.B. He seems now to be less determined to cut himself off completely. He's hedging a bit on just how much of a hermit he really wants to be.

Holden is about to receive another shock that may bring him even closer to the reality that he's been trying so hard to avoid. It comes at the climax of his conversation with Phoebe in front of the museum.

Instead of coming to meet him right from school, Phoebe went home and packed some of her belongings so she could run away with her brother. She now refuses to listen to any plan of his that doesn't include her. After insisting over and over again that she isn't going back to school, she tells Holden to shut up.

"It was the first time she ever told me to shut up," Holden says. "It sounded terrible. God, it sounded terrible. It sounded worse than swearing."

The night before, Holden ignored her acting as though she were his older sister. But he can't ignore her telling him to shut up. It looks as though Holden has seen the first sign that his little sister is growing up. Holden doesn't want to see *anyone* grow up, especially not Phoebe.. How does he deal with this potentially earth-shaking fact? Read what he says a little later about Phoebe's grabbing for the gold ring on the carousel:

"I was sort of afraid she'd fall off the goddam horse," he says, "but I didn't say anything or do anything. The thing with kids is, if they want to grab for the gold ring, you have to let them do it, and not say anything. If they fall off, they fall off, but it's bad if you say anything to them."

That sounds as though Holden has learned an important truth about innocence and childhood: that neither is a permanent condition. "It's bad if you say anything to them," he says, signifying that he realizes that you can't stop someone from moving into another stage of life.

He may have finally come to grips with his fear of seeing people grow up and change. He is, after all, admitting that he can't stop Phoebe from doing it, and Phoebe represents everything he has been trying to preserve. This sudden realization of a truth seems to have a good effect on Holden. He tells us he "felt so damn happy all of a sudden."

And that's the first time in the book he's been happy about anything.

CHAPTER 26

The Catcher in the Rye has much in common with Mark Twain's *The Adventures of Huckleberry Finn*. One of the similarities is in their final chapters.

Huck closes by saying that if he had known how much trouble it would be to write a book, he never would have tried it. At the end of the story he's dissatisfied, as though the telling didn't accomplish much.

Holden seems to be echoing Huck's sentiment. "I'm sorry I told so many people about it," he says. ". . . Don't ever tell anybody anything. If you do, you start missing everybody."

Chapter 25 ended with Holden apparently having resolved his fear of seeing his loved ones change and grow. That's certainly a positive sign. But in the closing chapter, Holden says things that remind us of other aspects of his emotional problem.

We saw him constantly having trouble communicating with people. Now that he's told his story, he says he thinks the telling was pointless. That isn't a good sign.

We saw that Holden had trouble fitting into the world he lived in, especially in school. Now he tells us he has no idea how he's going to "apply" himself when he returns to school.

We saw that he tends to minimize serious problems, probably in an attempt to keep from having to face them. Now when D.B. asks him what he thinks about what has happened, he says he doesn't know. He still isn't ready to seriously analyze what's bothering him.

To the question, "Has Holden changed?" the answer would seem to be, "Well, yes and no." His realization that Phoebe will grow up is a big step for him. His tempering of the daydream to leave the world he knows is a sign that he may be ready to try adapting to that world.

On the other hand, he still can't see any value in communicating with people, he still anticipates trouble in school, and he still won't face his problems.

What has happened to Holden? And what will happen to him in the near future? In the distant future? As a careful reader of the novel, you're as qualified to answer those questions as anyone else.

A STEP BEYOND

Tests and Answers

TESTS

Test 1

1. The title refers to Holden Caulfield's wish to _____
   A. protect children
   B. imitate his dead brother Allie
   C. prove his worth to his parents

2. Which is *not* true of the novel? _____
   A. It is narrated in the first person
   B. The actions of the hero are more important than his thoughts
   C. It is told in a flashback

3. Holden feels that _____
   A. Antolini is his only adult friend
   B. his brother D.B. has "prostituted" himself in Hollywood
   C. James Castle was wrong to commit suicide

4. The novel opens and closes _____
   A. in Pencey Prep in Pennsylvania
   B. in Holden's home in New York
   C. in a "rest home" in California

5. More than anything else, Holden hates _____
   A. old people
   B. phonies
   C. baseball players

6. Which pair of characters play similar roles in Holden's life? _____

A. Phoebe and Sally Hayes
B. Spencer and Antolini
C. Carl Luce and Jane Gallagher

7. Holden is beaten up by ____
A. Ward Stradlater and Maurice
B. Ackley
C. the taxi driver

8. There is irony in ____
A. Holden's love for Phoebe and his refusal to take her with him
B. Holden's contempt for movies and his apparent familiarity with films
C. Holden's expulsion from school and his excellent grades

9. Which is true of Holden? ____
A. He respects Mr. Ossenburger for his philanthropy
B. He feels the red hat brings him luck
C. He likes an author whom you would feel like telephoning

10. Holden does not go directly home from Pencey Prep because ____
A. he is afraid to face his parents until school officially closes for the holidays
B. he is anxious for a few days of freedom in New York
C. he is seriously considering going out West

11. What is Holden's attitude toward Jane Gallagher, and why is it an important part of the novel?

12. What does Phoebe stand for in Holden's mind?

13. Why is Holden so concerned about the ducks on the lake in Central Park?

14. What is Holden's attitude toward girls, and what does this attitude say about him?
15. What is Holden's attitude toward religion, and what does this attitude say about him?

Test 2

1. A question that is on Holden's mind and is the subject of several conversations is ____
   A. Why did the children in the museum choose to visit the Egyptian mummies?
   B. What happens to the ducks in Central Park during the winter?
   C. Why aren't the exhibits in the American Museum of Natural History changed more often?

2. According to Holden, Ernie the piano player, the Lunts, and Laurence Olivier ____
   A. confuse art and entertainment
   B. are the best performers in their respective fields
   C. leave him cold

3. "Then all of a sudden, I got in this big mess" introduces the episode ____
   A. of Holden's expulsion from school
   B. of his drunkenness at the hotel
   C. of his encounter with the prostitute

4. After Maurice and Sonny leave Holden, ____
   A. he considers suicide but rejects it in favor of revenge
   B. he counts his money to see how much they have stolen
   C. he fantasizes that he has been shot

5. The meeting with the nuns reminds Holden of ____

A. his change of heart about religion
B. an incident with his roommate's suitcase at Elkton Hills School
C. his loneliness and estrangement from his family

6. Holden buys a record for Phoebe and ____
A. brings it home to her although it is broken
B. loses it at Grand Central Station
C. apologizes to her for such a meager gift

7. Holden's date with Sally ends ____
A. with an innocent kiss
B. in an argument
C. with his proposing to her

8. Holden says, ____
A. "Maybe all bores have some secret talent"
B. "I hate when kids ask you to tighten their skates for them"
C. "It's depressing to think I'll probably end up a lawyer like my father"

9. Holden shows he may have arrived at a point of maturity when he ____
A. determines to "make it" on his own
B. decides to return home with Phoebe
C. says he will never miss the people he has been talking about

10. Which is *not* true of Phoebe? ____
A. She lies to her mother about smoking
B. She gives Holden all her money
C. She is frightened of the carousel

11. How does Holden feel about his parents?

12. Discuss Holden's failed attempts to communicate with people.
13. Discuss the importance of Allie in Holden's life.
14. How typical do you think Holden Caulfield is?
15. Draw a character sketch of Holden at twenty-five or thirty years old.

ANSWERS

Test 1

1. A 2. B 3. B 4. C 5. B 6. B
7. A 8. B 9. C 10. A

11. There's no doubt that Jane is special to Holden, and that her special status is closely related to her vulnerability and insecurity. But before you write anything about her, look beyond these relatively obvious statements. An essay about Jane should touch on most of the following questions: Why does Holden keep talking about calling her? Why does he hesitate for so long before actually doing it? What would he have said to her if she had answered the phone? How would she have reacted to him? Why does he stop talking about her at the end of the book? (The last mention of Jane is in Mr. Antolini's apartment.)

12. Remember that Phoebe is much more than just a child (although that would be enough for Holden). She's a very bright child; she's also sensitive, amusing, and articulate. In an essay dealing with her importance to Holden, you should deal with any contrast you see between Phoebe in the real world and Phoebe in Holden's mind. How much of his private Phoebe is an idealization? How much is the result of his freezing her at a certain point in her life? And don't forget the unique circumstance that makes Phoebe different from every other child Holden knows: she knew Allie in the same intimate way he did.

13. As the comments on individual chapters pointed out repeatedly, Holden's preoccupation is with defenseless and vulnerable people. The ducks, of course, symbolize this concern, but simply stating that wouldn't produce a very satisfactory essay. You would want to show evidence of Holden's preoccupation with the ducks. You might also analyze the two conversations he has with cab drivers about the ducks, and how his comments in those conversations reflect his attitude toward the ducks.

14. Holden tends to think of girls as defenseless, in need of his protection. He feels this way even when he's with someone who would laugh at the suggestion that he could protect her. (Reread his conversation with Sunny, the prostitute who comes to his hotel room.) This feeling extends even to women. He feels protective of his mother; of Mrs. Morrow, the woman he meets on the train from Pencey; and of the two nuns he has breakfast with. Jane Gallagher may be the epitome of the helpless female (in Holden's mind, at least), but she's certainly not the only one in his universe. In dealing with this question, you might give some attention to whether Holden's attitude toward girls changes by the end of the book.

15. Holden has some very definitive, and very funny, things to say about organized religion. But you don't want to deal with a question like this without distinguishing between organized religion and religious feelings. Holden's objections to organized religion go right to the source: he doesn't much like the disciples, who were the first organizers of Christianity. He does, however, have a high regard for Jesus, who represents true religious feelings and impulses. Holden calls himself an atheist because he doesn't practice any form of organized religion, and because the God his society believes in doesn't seem real to him. But his talking to Allie is a form of prayer, and other things he says suggest a religious feeling that may not be satisfied by the organized religions he has come in contact with. An essay on his attitude toward religion should deal with most of these topics.

Test 2

1. B 2. A 3. C 4. C 5. B 6. A
7. B 8. A 9. B 10. C

11. One clue begins with the second sentence of the novel. But you'll have to go over the book carefully to find most of the other remarks Holden makes about his parents. He mentions his mother more often than his father, and we even see his mother in the scene with Phoebe. But he suggests a great deal about his father when Phoebe asks him what he wants to be when he finishes school. You'll have to integrate these references to plan an essay on this question.

12. It would probably be a good idea to narrow your subject. One way to do that is to list all the people Holden talks to during the story, then to select four or five characters who have something in common. You can then use this common thread to tie your essay together. You could, for example, write only about the strangers Holden tries to talk with—Mrs. Morrow, the two cab drivers, the three women at the bar. Or you could write only about conversations that end in hostility, like those with Ackley, Stradlater, the three women, Sally Hayes, and Carl Luce. Another thing to remember about a general question like this one is that it doesn't suggest what point you should make in your essay. That's another thing you should decide before you start writing. An essay about Holden's failed attempts to communicate might point out that the failure is often his fault, or that it's always funny, or that it shows how sick he is.

13. In preparing an essay on Allie you should reread at least three sections of the book: Holden's first mention of his brother, when he writes the composition for Stradlater; his conversation about Allie with Phoebe; and his plea to Allie during the emotional crisis that arises just before he meets Phoebe at the museum. When you put all these together (and add Holden's other references to Allie), you'll see that Allie is more than a memory, more than a well-loved brother, even more than a symbol of childhood innocence. He has a religious significance in Holden's life, and any essay on Allie should mention this.

14. This is the kind of question that calls as much on your personal experience as it does on your reading of the novel. The best way to prepare an essay answer is to collect dozens of quotes from the novel to support your opinion. Your essay will have some strength if your statement is backed up by his references to disappearing, to falling, and to not being able to cope. Once you've established what Holden is like, your next job is to give some evidence for what most people his age are like. These two parts of your essay will then be the basis for your overall conclusion that Holden is or is not typical of American teenagers.

15. Since the assignment asks you to be creative, there's obviously no "right" answer. There is, however, a right way to approach this kind of essay. It involves accumulating evidence from Holden's words and trying to project from that evidence the kind of adult the speaker might become. You might also separate his opinions into two groups: those that will take a more adult form in ten or fifteen years, and those that Holden will have to discard as he grows older. If you're feeling really creative, you could write this essay in Holden's voice as an adult.

Term Paper Ideas

1. Compare Holden to Huckleberry Finn in terms of self-image, language, and attitude toward society.

2. Compare Holden to the main character of Stephen Crane's *The Red Badge of Courage.*

3. Analyze Salinger's success at writing comic dialogue.

4. Explain why you think the novel is optimistic or pessimistic.

5. Show how Holden's many references to movies reveal something about him.

6. Discuss Holden's comments about artists, such as the Lunts, Laurence Olivier, and Ernie the piano player.

7. Discuss Holden's comments about sex.

8. Show how Holden is not as mature or sophisticated as he would like people to believe.

9. Discuss the various definitions of *phony* Holden uses throughout the book.

10. Discuss the use of sports imagery in the book, including Holden's red hunting hat.

11. If you've read any of the books Holden mentions, discuss his opinion of the book(s).

12. Describe the differences in Holden in the three sections of the novel. (See the section on Form and Structure.)

13. Evaluate Holden's attitude toward children.

14. Analyze the changes in Holden's speech patterns when he's talking to certain adults in the novel.

15. Discuss the importance of Central Park in the novel.

16. Analyze the relationship between Holden and Phoebe, as it shows itself in her bedroom and at the end of the novel.

17. Discuss Holden's attitude toward material possessions.

18. Contrast the conversation Holden has with Mr. Spencer and the one he has with Mr. Antolini.

19. Show how the weekend Holden tells us about is related to his daydreams about living in a monastery and on the edge of the woods.

20. Explain Holden's attitude toward successful lawyers, and show what this reveals about him.

21. Explain why you think Holden does or does not belong in the hospital or rest home from which he's telling the story.

22. Discuss the differences in Holden's attitude toward Phoebe, Allie, and Jane Gallagher.

23. Show how Holden's flair for lying is or is not helpful to him in conversations.

24. Describe a school or educational system that Holden would find appealing.

25. Describe three different people—his own age or older—that Holden would enjoy spending time with.

Further Reading

CRITICAL WORKS

Belcher, William F., and James W. Lee, eds. *J. D. Salinger and the Critics*. Belmont, Calif.: Wadsworth, 1962.

French, Warren. *J. D. Salinger*. New York: Twayne, 1963.

Galloway, David D. *The Absurd Hero in American Fiction*. Austin: University of Texas Press, 1966.

Grunwald, Henry A., ed. *Salinger: A Critical and Personal Portrait*. New York: Harper & Row, 1962.

Gwynn, Frederick L., and Joseph Blotner. *The Fiction of J. D. Salinger*. Pittsburgh: University of Pittsburgh Press, 1964.

Laser, Marvin, and Norman Fruman, eds. *Studies in J. D. Salinger*. New York: Odyssey, 1963.

Rosen, Gerald. *Zen in the Art of J. D. Salinger*. Berkeley: Creative Arts, 1977.

AUTHOR'S OTHER WORKS

Nine Stories (1953)
Franny and Zooey (1961)
Raise High the Roof Beam, Carpenters and Seymour: An Introduction (1963)

Before the publication of *The Catcher in the Rye*, Salinger published a number of stories that have not been collected in an authorized edition. These stories appeared from 1940 to 1948 in the magazines *Collier's*, *Saturday Evening Post*, *Cosmopolitan*, *Story*, *Esquire*, *Mademoiselle*, and *Good Housekeeping*. One of the stories, "I'm Crazy," included passages that Salinger later used in *The Catcher in the Rye*. It appeared in the December 22, 1945, issue of *Collier's*. A complete list of Salinger's stories, with their dates of publication, is in Warren French's *J.D. Salinger*.

The Critics

On Jane

What he especially liked about Jane was that in checkers she kept her kings in the back row. This has intrigued the critics, but what it seems to represent is a holding back of one's aggressive powers and an unwillingness to enter the competitive game and use them against other people; this is one of Holden's cherished values, and in his case, his bane as well.

—*Gerald Rosen,*
Zen in the Art of J. D. Salinger, *1977*

Holden and Huck Finn

This novel's exciting resemblances to *The Adventures of Huckleberry Finn* have been justly noted by a number of critics—the comic irony, the colloquial language, the picaresque structure and the theme of anti-phoniness and it is not inconceivable that someday Holden Caulfield may be as well known an American boy as Huck Finn. For a reader goes through much the same pattern of relishing both boys: first it is the release provided by their rebellion from society, then the inspiration of their honesty against sham, and then the sympathetic awareness of their melancholy roles.

—*Frederick L. Gwynn and Joseph Blotner,*
The Fiction of J. D. Salinger, *1964*

Salinger's Love of Children

Holden can only find genuine love in children, who have not learned the deadening rituals of pretense.

—*Dan Wakefield, in Henry A. Grunwald,*
Salinger, A Critical and Personal Portrait, *1962*

In one of his few published comments, Salinger has said of *The Catcher:* "I'm aware that many of my friends will be saddened and shocked, or shocked-saddened, over some of the chapters in *The Catcher in the Rye*. Some of my best friends are children. In fact, all my best friends are children. It's almost unbearable for me to realize that my book will be kept on a shelf out of their reach."

—*David Leitch, in Henry A. Grunwald,* Salinger, A Critical and Personal Portrait, *1962*

The Need to Love

The response of these outsiders (Holden and Phoebe, for instance) to the dull or angry world about them is not simply one of withdrawal: it often takes the form of a strange quixotic gesture. The gesture, one feels for sure, is the bright metaphor of Salinger's sensibility, the center from which meaning derives and ultimately the reach of his commitment to past innocence and current guilt. . . . There is often something prodigal and spontaneous about it, something humorous or whimsical, something that disrupts our habits of gray acquiescence and revives our faith in the willingness of the human spirit. But above all, it gives as only a *religious* gesture can. . . . In another age, Cervantes endowed Don Quixote with the capacity to perform it and so did Twain and Fitzgerald endow their best creations . . . the young man who insists on giving half a chicken sandwich to a stranger.

—*Ihab Hassan, in Henry A. Grunwald,* Salinger, A Critical and Personal Portrait, *1962*

Holden and Society

In the epilogue to the novel Holden suggests the possibility of re-entering society when he says, "I sort of miss everybody I told you about. Even old Stradlater and Ackley, for instance. I think I even miss that goddam Maurice." Holden misses even the phonies of the world because his experience has taught him something about the necessity of loving, and here Salinger sounds what is to become his major and most complex theme.

—*David D. Galloway,*
The Absurd Hero in American Fiction, *1966*

A Lyric Monologue

The Catcher in the Rye, despite its brilliance of observation and the virtuosity with which Salinger keeps Holden Caulfield's monologue going for the length of a novel, is primarily concerned neither with the working out of a plot nor the development of a character. It is a lyric monologue in which the complex feelings of an essentially static character are revealed. For all Salinger's skill, *The Catcher in the Rye* has a claustrophobic and, at the same time, random quality.

—*Arthur Mizener, in Henry A. Grunwald,*
Salinger, A Critical and Personal Portrait, *1962*

A Portrait of Ourselves

Rather than wishing quarterly significance or "greatness" on him [Salinger], we can be content to take him for what he is: a beautifully deft, professional performer who gives us a chance to catch quick, half-amused, half-frightened glimpses of ourselves and our contemporaries, as he confronts us with his brilliant mirror images.

—*David L. Stevenson, in Henry A. Grunwald,*
Salinger, A Critical and Personal Portrait, *1962*

Salinger, the Outsider

The only thing that Salinger does not do for this audience is to meet with them. Holden Caulfield said in *The Catcher in the Rye* that "What really knocks me out is a book that, when you're all done reading it, you wish the author that wrote it was a terrific friend of yours and you could call him up on the phone whenever you felt like it." It is well for him that all the people in this country who now regard J. D. Salinger as a "terrific friend" do not call him up and reach him.

—*Alfred Kazin, "J. D. Salinger: Everybody's Favorite,"* The Atlantic Monthly, *August 1961*